On Truth
An Ontological Theory

On Truth
An Ontological Theory

ELIOT DEUTSCH

The University Press of Hawaii 🛈
Honolulu

Manufactured in the United States of America

Library of Congress Cataloging in Publication Data

Deutsch, Eliot.
  On truth, an ontological theory.

  Bibliography: p.
  1. Truth. 2. Ontology. I. Title.
BD171.D37   111.8′3   79–12754
ISBN 0–8248–0615–8

For Adley

Contents

Acknowledgments

MY INDEBTEDNESS to many colleagues and friends for their advice, criticism, and encouragement during the preparation of this work is very great indeed. With the gracious financial assistance of the *National Endowment for the Humanities* under its Senior Fellowship program (1973–1974), I was given the opportunity to develop many of the ideas in this work, especially on art, and to present some of these ideas in meetings with colleagues in Europe and Asia. I have benefited enormously from these discussions. I have also had the good fortune to receive criticisms and suggestions from my colleague Irving Copi and from David T. Wieck. I am particularly indebted to the students and faculty of the Perkins School of Theology and the Department of Philosophy at Southern Methodist University for inviting me to give a series of lectures on the topic of truth in the spring of 1975. Questions and criticisms raised were most helpful in sharpening up some of the material. My greatest debt, however, for the theory of truth elaborated here is to my students in a graduate seminar on the problem of truth held at the University of Hawaii. What the students in the seminar taught me on the subject is I hope evident in this work.

An earlier version of part of the material in chapter 1 was published in the *Journal of Chinese Philosophy* 3 (1976): 373–397. I am grateful to the editor, Chung-ying Cheng, for permission to incorporate the material in this study. Portions of chapter 3 first appeared in *Self, Knowledge and Freedom: Essays for Kalidas Bhattacharyya,* edited by I. N. Mohanty and S. P. Banerjee (Calcutta: World Press Private Limited, 1978).

"What is truth?" Pilate asks;
And Hegel answers:
    "Truth is not a minted coin which can be given
    and pocketed ready-made."

    Preface to the *Phenomenology* 3, no. 1

On Truth
An Ontological Theory

Introduction

IN THE LATIN *veritas,* the Sanskrit *satya,* the Arabic *ḥaqq,* "truth" and "reality" are closely identified. Truth is not just a property of statements, propositions, or beliefs; it is a quality of being, of human beings and human activities. In the English language, on the other hand, the word "truth" (or "true") is used quite explicitly in at least three basic ways: (1) as the manner in which things are in themselves or the manner in which the world is in itself; truth as reality, truth as being—*truth as opposed to nonbeing or the purely fictional;* (2) as genuineness of a thing—'Yeats is a true poet'; 'These are true pearls'; truth as the conformity of the thing to our idea, definition, or conception of the thing—*truth as opposed to the counterfeit, the fake;* and (3) as a property of a statement, proposition, or belief, usually as the linguistic or mental entity is thought to correspond to or with what is in fact the case—*truth as opposed to the erroneous, the false.*

Now, in recent decades, especially under the impact of positivism, which led philosophers to make a sharp division between cognitive meaning (basically having to do with declarative sentences which assert empirically verifiable propositions) and emotive meaning (various forms of imperatives and the like that may bear expressive value), "truth" has come more and more to be narrowly restricted to logical truth-value, to propositions, with all other forms and usages of "truth" taken to be metaphorical, to have significance only by virtue of their striking a bargain, as it were, with propositional truth. This restriction of the application, and narrowing of the meaning, of "truth," however, I believe, is wrong and unfortunate; for it robs the concept of some of its richest possible meaning.

I propose that we start our thinking about the nature of truth—

about what truth is—by looking first to our aesthetic and religious experience. I propose that we ask first 'What sense of "truth" is appropriate to artworks and to religious language?'; from these analyses to develop a new conception about propositional truth (aiming to avoid at least some of the apparently insuperable difficulties in traditional and contemporary correspondence, coherence, pragmatic, redundancy, performative, and semantic theories); and finally to formulate a general, unified notion of truth which may apply to all its varied forms and kinds. I propose, in other words, that we reverse the usual direction of inquiry into the meaning of truth by starting with (i.e., finding the appropriate meaning of) "truth" in art and in religious language, and then in propositional language, ending with a general theory of truth.

Now this proposed redirection in our thinking about truth obviously has roots in, or affinities with, other ontological approaches; and to help locate the thinking about truth presented here it might be useful to sketch critically, and very briefly, a few of these other approaches. Foremost, perhaps, among them is that of Hegel's effort to work out a conception of truth in keeping with his "absolute Idealism." According to Hegel, the essence of truth has to do with the conformity of a thing to its concept or notion *(Begriff)*. Distinguishing rather sharply between "correctness" *(Richtigkeit)*—or that "correspondence" which most philosophers take to be the right sense of truth—and "truth" proper, Hegel, in his *Logic,* writes:

> In common life the terms *truth* and *correctness* are often treated as synonymous: we speak of the truth of a content, when we are only thinking of its correctness. Correctness, generally speaking, concerns only the formal coincidence between our conception and its content, whatever the constitution of this content may be. Truth, on the contrary, lies in the coincidence of the object with itself, that is, with its notion *[Begriff]*. That a person is sick, or that someone has committed a theft, may certainly be correct. But the content is untrue. A sick body is not in harmony with the notion of body. . . .[1]

The "notion" of a thing, for Hegel, is the essential, defining quality of a thing; what the thing is supposed to be in our conception of it.

As in the ancient Confucian doctrine of "the rectification of names," things, for Hegel, are properly themselves only when they are what they should be according to their nature as they are conceived. And thus, in his *Phenomenology of Mind,* Hegel is able to say that "truth finds the medium of its existence in notions and conceptions alone."[2] Hegel's *Begriff,* though, has something of the Platonic-Aristotelian 'form' about it insofar as it is a kind of standard, model, or perfection for the thing. Hegel says:

> When thus viewed, to be untrue means much the same as to be bad. The bad man is an untrue man, a man who does not behave as his notion or his vocation requires.[3]

Judgments are true, then, according to Hegel, to the degree to which their content represents the conformity of a thing to its notion. Truth becomes a matter of degree; for, within the larger metaphysical schema wherein truth has its meaning, one determines the truth of something relative to the advancement of Spirit, the Absolute, as it moves dialectically toward its own self-conscious completion.

> The truth is the whole. The whole, however, is merely the essential nature reaching its completeness through the process of its own development. Of the Absolute it must be said that it is essentially a result, that only at the end is it what it is in very truth. . . .[4]

Now for this union of the particular and the general, this "concrete universal" which expresses the Absolute, to be possible Hegel employs the concept of the Idea *(Idée)*—the rational structure of reality. Charles Taylor, in his recent work on Hegel, explains that

> 'The Idea is true which is *an und für sich.*' For truth . . . is that reality be in agreement with its concept, with the concept which produces it. But the concept producing a reality and bringing it into agreement with it, this is the Idea.[5]

The Idea, then, is grasped in a concept or notion, but nevertheless extends beyond it. Stanley Rosen explains Hegel's position thus:

> The Idea is the "adequate concept" or objective truth about the formation process of the Absolute. In traditional epistemological language, it

is the adequacy of the concept to the object. But Hegel's "Idea" is not the expression of a "correspondence theory" of truth, because the adequacy of the concept arises from its coherence with the object. For Hegel, to think the truth is to be "in the truth," or still more sharply, *to be* the truth. . . . As the truth, the Idea is thus unconditioned. It is the Whole: there is nothing outside it. . . .[6]

Hegel saw clearly the importance of the relationship between truth and reality. Objects, and not just propositions about them, may be said to be true—and to be in truth to the degree to which they bear the presence, as it were, of that integrated process of conscious-reality which Hegel calls the Absolute. Hegel thus must be credited for the profound insight that truth is not something that is simply delivered whole and complete by a proposition as such but rather requires a *process* in which the object that may bear a truth realizes itself as the thing that it properly is.

Hegel's conception of truth, however, suffers various deficiencies. Apart from the questionable rationalistic monism which underlies it, his conception makes for an unresolved cleavage between "correctness," or the usual correspondence sense of truth, and ontological coherence; and, perhaps more importantly, it presupposes that things have notions which are somehow separable from, that is, may be determined conceptually (albeit they may not be realized existentially) externally to, their concrete particularity. A "sick body" may indeed, under appropriate conditions and circumstances, be seen as what is right for a person and be a contributing factor (condition) to the truth of his being. The 'notion' of a thing, we will need and want to argue, is not a preexistent concept or form, but what the individual thing itself aims to be precisely in terms of what the individual thing itself is. The concept of "appropriateness" must, we will argue, be of crucial importance in formulating a conception of truth which involves the rightness of a thing.

Tracing the concept of truth back to its early Greek origins as *aletheia*, "unconcealedness," Martin Heidegger, in his now classic *Being and Time,* argues that truth is a *discovery,* a "showing-forth" of an object, of what he calls an *essent.* J. L. Mehta, in language somewhat less dense than Heidegger's, explicates the teaching in this way:

> What perception establishes is nothing other than *that* it actually *is* the essent itself which was meant in the statement, that the statement-making relation to what is stated is a shining forth of the essent, that it *discovers* the essent about which it is. What is evidenced is the discovering character of the statement. The essent meant in the judgment shows itself so as it is in itself; it is in itself so as the statement shows forth or discovers it to be.[7]

Heidegger's theory, it is said, is neither a "correspondence" nor a "coherence" theory; it is rather an ontological theory insofar as it emphasizes the *essent* in *unconcealedness.* Heidegger's thinking about truth, though, is given perhaps its clearest and most mature formulation in his 1930 essay "Vom Wesen der Wahrheit" ("On the Essence of Truth"), where, while retaining the idea of *aletheia,* he argues that the essence of truth (as "correspondence") is freedom.

Heidegger first takes up the "conventional" concept of truth and sees it in its dual aspect of "the correspondence of a thing with the idea of it as conceived in advance *(dem über sie Vorgemeinten),* and secondly the correspondence of that which is intended by the statement with the thing itself."[8] The traditional (medieval) definition— *veritas est adaequatio rei et intellectus*—brings out, according to Heidegger, this dual aspect of correspondence. He points out, though, that this is based on "the Christian theological belief that things are only what they are, if they are, to the extent that they, as created things *(ens creatum)* correspond to an *idea* preconceived in the *intellectus divinus,* that is to say, in the mind of God, and thus conform to the idea (are right) and are in this sense 'true'."[9] Heidegger goes on then to stress that "Truth does not possess its original seat in the proposition."[10]

> All behaviour is "overt" (lit. "stands open": *offenständig*) to what-is, and all "overt" relationship is behaviour. Man's "overtness" varies with the nature of what-is and the mode of behaviour. All working and carrying out of tasks, all transaction and calculation, sustains itself in the

open, an overt region within which what-is can expressly take up its stand *as* and *how* it is *what* it is, and thus become capable of expression. This can only occur when what-is represents itself *(selbst vorstellig wird)* with the representative statement, so that the statement submits to a directive enjoining it to express what-is "such as" or just as it is.[11]

He goes on to say that

But if rightness (truth) of statement is only made possible by the overt character of behaviour, then it follows that the thing that makes rightness possible in the first place must have a more original claim to be regarded as the essence of truth.[12]

And that

The overt character of behaviour in the sense that it makes rightness a possibility, is grounded in freedom. *The essence of truth is freedom.*[13]

Heidegger explains that " 'Essence' is understood here as the basis of the inner possibility of whatever is accepted in the first place and generally admitted as 'known'."[14] The freedom which is the essence of truth, for Heidegger, is thus not a freedom for caprice or for mere invention; rather, "the freedom to reveal something overt lets whatever 'is' at the moment *be* what it is. Freedom reveals itself as the 'letting-be' of what is."[15] This "letting-be" is not indifference or neglect, Heidegger insists; it is, once again, a positive uncovering of what is: truth is *aletheia,* the unconcealment of being.

Now, apart from the enormous obscurities in Heidegger's writing on truth, it is clear, I think, that Heidegger is concerned primarily to point us in the direction of seeing the intimate relationship that obtains between reality and truth. The truth of a thing makes sense to him, as it ought to us, and he sees this truth as related to a standing forth of a thing in an unconcealed openness. Propositions must intend to uncover what is as it is; they must aim to be revelatory.

Yet for all of Heidegger's striking originality, it doesn't seem that his conception of truth is a radical breaking away from the conventional (correspondence) position. Heidegger is looking more for the essence of the conventional sense, rather than seeking to frame a new conception of truth as such. Mehta acknowledges as much when he says that the "interpretation of truth as being discovering is neither arbitrary nor does it throw overboard the good old tradition, as it might at first appear, but is only the necessary explication of what was foreshadowed in it.''[16]

For a somewhat more radical break in the formulation of an ontological approach to truth we must turn to the thought of the contemporary American philosopher Albert Hofstadter.

In developing his theory of truth Hofstadter builds explicitly on the foundations laid by Hegel and Heidegger. He distinguishes three kinds of truth: *truth of statement* (propositional truth), *truth of things,* and *truth of spirit.* Truth of statement, the first kind, is a *cognitive* order of truth having to do with the adequacy of thought or language to thing. Following Aristotle's definition,[17] Hofstadter sees truth of statement as essentially a matter of correspondence:

> As applied to language, the cognitive ideal is the adequation of the language to the thing it speaks about, in such a way that it says of what is that it is and what is not that it is not. This ideal is the ideal of propositional truth or truth of statement.[18]

Hofstadter goes on to sum up approvingly Heidegger's understanding of this conventional, correspondence concept of truth as an ''uncovering'':

> We might therefore say that statement, as such, articulates a human aiming at what-is. This aiming is an attempt at or an effort after the uncovering of what-is. If the effort succeeds, so that the intended entity is selfsame with the real entity, the statement is true. It uncovers the entity; the intention, transcending itself, reaches its destination; or, *vice versa,* on reaching its destination, it uncovers the entity, bringing it into the openness of human being.[19]

> The concept of truth of statement as outlined above is essentially the correspondence concept, where the conformity is understood in its ideal sense as identity of intended and existent.[20]

Preparing the way for a dialectical ordering of the relations between the three kinds of truth, Hofstadter notes that

> A sacrifice, however, must be made for this blessing of the knowledge of truth, namely, the laying down of the self's will as self. In order to know truth, the self, as a being in the world, must take the form of an intend-

ing of entities in which its aim is to identify itself in intention, as far as possible, with the existent. The self, therefore, must become an intention identical with what is not itself. It must abandon any effort to be on its own account in order to be an intending of what-is in the form of what-is as such.[21]

The second kind of truth, truth of things, is characterized by Hofstadter as "the adequation of the thing to the intellect."

Unlike the cognitive ideal of the *understanding* of existence, it is the ideal of the *governance* of existence. If in cognition the self yields itself to existence, in practice the self demands that existence should yield itself to it.[22]

The truth of things is thus a human-willed truth: the conformity of the thing to our concept of it is essentially *imposed* upon the thing.

Within that field [of vision opened up by the concept of truth of things] there lies whatever the human will may wish to apply its own concept to, requiring of it that it subordinate itself to that concept.[23]

Hofstadter then sharply contrasts truth of statement and truth of things clearly in these terms:

Whereas in statement-truth the statement is required to direct itself toward identity of what it intends with the thing itself, now in thing-truth the thing itself is required to direct itself (or be directed) toward identity with what the willed idea intends. In both forms of truth there is identity of intended content and actual thing. In statement-truth, man, as understanding, seeks to conform himself *via* this identity to existence. In thing-truth, man, as will, *via* this identity, requires existence to conform to himself.[24]

But thing-truth, too, has its limitations, for it is *subject to* its own compelling "ought":

Here, too, as in the cognitive life, there is a *split* introduced, not just between the ought and the is of thing-truth in general, but between an ought and an is in the very being of man that constitutes him as practical in his relation to existence. For in practice, i.e. in so far as he exists as the aim at governance, man finds his own *actual* being subjected to an *ought,* namely, the ought-to-govern. And just as, in understanding, the aim at uncovering is generated from within, not imposed on man from without, so here in practical life the aim at governing issues spontaneously from man's own being. To be man, he must attempt to govern things in the world. But in this attempt to set himself up as governor, he already subjects his own self to an ought, the ought-to-govern, that belongs to him as human. . . .[25]

Hofstadter then goes on to ask if a truth of spirit is possible; one which will take up and complete the truths of statement and thing.

. . . here we are asking about the possibility of truth that encompasses the nature of the two previous forms of truth within itself. But this means that we are asking about the possibility of a mode of human existence that encompasses the two previous forms of existence within itself. Man exists as the aim to uncover the existent. Now we ask whether and how it is possible for man to exist in such a way as to comprehend both uncovering and governing, both understanding and will, in the unity of a new truth.[26]

His answer is affirmative: there is indeed a "truth of spirit" which involves "the mutual adequation of intellect and thing." And Hofstadter finds its primary philosophical locus in the thought of Hegel.

The most elaborate version of the nature of truth in the third sense, truth of spirit, is to be found in the philosophy of Hegel.[27]

Although Hofstadter rejects the metaphysics of Hegelian thought as it becomes "a gigantic (not to say monstrous) monistic metaphysical process of the evolution of a single, total divine self,"[28] he affirms what he takes to be the central insight of Hegel into the meaning of truth.

In statement-truth our concept directs itself toward intentional unity with the thing as it is in itself. In thing-truth, the thing is intended by our concept to be as that concept requires it to be. Now, in the third sense of truth, there is a new identity. In both the other forms stress was laid on the fact that the concept was *our* concept. In the third form it must equally—and indeed first of all—be the *thing's* concept. (Hence the thing itself must be intentionalistic.) For in this form of truth the thing is to be uncovered as being what it ought to be in and of itself, which can be the case only if the concept is the thing's own; and it is through this intrinsic character of the thing's own truth that *our* concept is led to identify itself with the thing's, or that we are brought to experience the truth of the thing as evidence of our thought and realization of our will.[29]

This is the sense of the definition of truth that Hegel repeats in every context and with regard to every aspect of existence: truth is the concrete unity of concept and objectivity.[30]

Except, of course, that Hegel disallows the possibility of separating out this "unity of concept and objectivity" from the Whole, the Idea, the Absolute:

. . . everything actual, in so far as it is true, is the Idea, and has its truth by and in virtue of the Idea alone. Every individual being is some one aspect of the Idea; for which, therefore, yet other actualities are needed, which in their turn appear to have a self-subsistence of their own. It is only in them altogether and in their relation that the notion is realised. The individual by itself does not correspond to its notion. It is this limitation of its existence which constitutes the finitude and the ruin of the individual.[31]

Hofstadter nevertheless applies—or evidences—this third kind of truth in his richly evocative analysis of art and concludes that

What is so clear in art, what is so innocent even in the most sophisticated art, is muddied and polluted in the stream of real existence, where we have to begin over again the search for the measure that brings human being into the eternally valid equipoise of the moment of truth.[32]

Now although we will differ in several crucial ways with Hofstadter's way of expressing the "truth of spirit," namely, with respect to what is meant by the *intention* of an object, the fundamental insight he articulates, that truth has to do with the realization of the object's own being, is, I believe, of great significance. It is the very essence of an ontological theory of truth.

We need to look clearly, and as deeply as we can, into the manner in which artworks, say, are able to achieve a rightness, a truth appropriate to their own intentionality. We need to understand, as best we can, how truth is realized concretely in a wide range of language usages through the articulation of their own aims. But to do this we do not so much need a "third kind" of truth that takes up, integrates, and completes propositional truth (of a correspondence kind) and the will-laden truth of things, as we need just a general, single conception of truth, which is derived primarily from an analysis of truth in art, in religious language, and in propositional language. Our conception of truth, in short, will have certain clear affinities with "truth of spirit" as understood by Hofstadter. It will not, however, involve a dialectical unfolding of different kinds of truth related to man's being in the world as knower and governor; it will, rather more simply, be a formulation of what we see as the meaning of truth derived from artworks (art), religious language (religion), and propositional language (philosophy). We will conclude that truth is an achievement of "rightness."

CHAPTER I
Truth in Art

IT IS ONE of the supreme ironies of the Western intellectual history that it is Plato (that consummate philosophical poet) who first introduces serious confusions about the relationship between truth and reality as it applies to art, confusions that center on his applying a simple correspondence-criterion of truth, which is drawn from a concern with truth of propositions (or ideas), to art. Plato (*Republic,* Bk. 10) finds the artist lacking powers of knowable insight and being thus reduced to making copies of objects which are themselves only poor reflections of their rational forms or Ideas. The copies do not correspond to, or conform with, reality. The poet (of the *Ion* and *Phaedrus*) is a kind of mad *demiurgos,* mind-lessly (without the employ of reason) making his world. For Plato there is no truth in art; the artist doesn't know whereof he speaks.[1]

Aristotle agrees with Plato that truth is essentially a matter of correspondence, but he finds truth to be somewhat irrelevant for art. According to Aristotle, "not to know that a hind has no horns is a less serious matter than to paint it inartistically."[2]

In Aesthetics, following Plato and Aristotle, the problem of truth in art has been formulated primarily in this context of accepting the primacy of propositional truth, and within that framework it has been repeatedly asked whether there is truth (of a propositional kind) in art and what, if any, its aesthetic relevance is.[3]

Albert Hofstadter, whose general theory of truth we have already outlined, has perhaps gone the furthest today in rethinking the idea of truth in art and in affirming art as an autonomous spiritual activity. Here following Susanne K. Langer (as well as Hegel and Heidegger), Hofstadter develops a new conception of what we mean by a work of art qua work being true. Truth in art is *sui generis*. The artistic symbol, he argues, is an *ontological* symbol.

> By this expression is meant a symbol which *is* essentially what it intends. The work of art *is,* as such, the entity that it intends. In this, it is unlike the symbol that occurs isolatedly in the context of truth of statement alone. A statement is not identical with what it intends.[4]

Now while I shall want to follow Hofstadter's lead in the direction of looking to the intentionality of the artwork as a basis for identifying its truth, truth in art is still being approached by Hofstadter from the initial standpoint of propositional truth ("truth of statement"), and this standpoint, we believe, needs to be "suspended," as it were, at the very beginning, so that the matter of truth in art may be resolved directly by the analysis of art and our experience of it.

Before we attempt to work out a somewhat more radical notion of, or look further for, truth in art, we need, then, to understand, and at some length (although necessarily in a somewhat sketchy and abstract manner, this being a work on truth and not in Aesthetics as such), what art is; and one way to understand what art is, which is to say, to formulate as far as possible a right conception of art, is to look to the origins of art in religion and to isolate, as far as one can, the most prominent features of the development of art as it moves from its beginnings in, and dependence upon, religion to its achieving its own autonomous integrity. This is not to say that the religious origins of art exhaust its genesis or ancestry (art, no doubt, also has origins in direct psychological needs for play, for expression, etc.), nor that any genetic account is more than a general schema whose value is more logical than historical; it is to say only that one might find something of essential importance about the nature of art by looking to its kinship with, and early dependence upon, religion. This, I believe, is not saying too much.

I

Gerardus van der Leeuw has pointed out convincingly how in "primitive" cultures, or at "the magical primitive stage" in any culture, the expressive forms of religious life—the drama, the hymn, the dance—are taken as centers of holy *power*. "There was a period," he writes, "—and for the so-called primitive peoples this period still exists—when art and religion stood so close to each other that they could almost be equated. Song was prayer; drama was divine performance; dance was cult."[5] Art, in short, was ritual—and was magical. The expressive forms generate and, at the same time, embody a spiritual energy that may radically transform whatever or whomever it touches.

Now, what any form of magic seeks is essentially control over the mysterious forces that are everywhere present in nature and life and that are potentially active in the affairs of man. By bringing the participant into unity with these forces, the rite, the consecrated act, allows the participant to take on directly something of this power so that it may express his own will. Consequently, the expressive forms of religious life—the dance, the chant—are not intended so much to be objects of disinterested contemplation (as supposedly works of art are) as to be carriers and bearers of *power*. It is the *holy power* inherent in the work (which power requires the action of the participant for its very being) which gives a particular work its special value.

When the art-religion work is a center of power, it thus expresses and contains, for those who respond to it properly, the immanence of the divine spirit. Literally lifeless in itself the work may be, and frequently is, discarded when not in use (as with certain African masks); that is, when it is not functioning so as to bring forth the immanent power of spirit. It is when the work is a holy or *consecrated* action that it exists as a center of power.

"Power" is spiritual force—a concentration of energy. Just as the ascetic in all cultures is thought to be capable of generating and containing a special superabundant energy (a kind of "heat" or *tapas*), one which in traditional Hindu lore may even, because of its intensity, threaten the gods, so the art-religion work, when performed or made correctly, is thought to manifest a sacred power. The power, at this stage, is just ritualistic—which is to say, it exists just so long as the art-religion work is being performed correctly; and it is also cosmic; it is grounded in, and is thought to be an "imitation" of, reality.

A second stage or moment of kinship between art and religion is to be found at the "traditional"[6] level of culture where, with the development of a conceptual theology, art-religion works are called upon to communicate ideas, concepts, and visions. The art-religion work becomes a bearer of symbols, usually of a conventional sort, and is, at its best, itself taken to function symbolically—to point beyond itself to yet other states of being. While still retaining many features of the power-oriented primitive, the traditional stage emphasizes the transcendent features of spirituality and sees in the now emerging artwork a means of communicating, of transmitting, a range of meanings associated with these features; for example, divine love and goodness. The artist is here very much a maker, a craftsman. He doesn't so much express himself or his own intuition as he projects a group or cult vision of reality.

In the famous "Dance of Śiva" *(Naṭarāja)* of Indian art, for example, Śiva, the Lord, exhibits through his great cosmic dance the power and rhythm that creates and sustains all life. Stamping out ignorance *(avidyā)*, which is symbolized by the dwarflike shape of the *apasmāra puruṣa*, Śiva also shows the way by which man can be released from the bondage of the world. The raised left foot signifies the giving of release, the drum creation, the flames of fire destruction. Everything in the work 'stands for' something else; the work can be understood, can be responded to properly, therefore, only when one knows what the symbols mean (i.e., are intended to stand for).

In the "traditional" relationship between art and religion, then, with its emphasis upon the work as symbol, we frequently find the subservience of aesthetic values to religious needs, especially when, as so often happened in the Western medieval period, the work was intended to be instructional in character. The *meaning* dimension, largely confined to the level of conventional symbolization, dominates. At this stage the meaning of the emerging artwork, then, is essentially *external* to the work. The message has already been formulated; it requires only representation or communication. The aesthetic is valued here insofar as it facilitates religious teaching.

Since the time of the Renaissance, with the artist emerging as a distinct, self-consciously *creative* being, we have come to separate art and religion in many ways.[7] We look to the artwork as it may be a direct embodiment of spirituality. It is not *power* or *meaning*, as these functioned in the "primitive" and "traditional" phases, but aesthetic *quality* that now counts and enables us to accept art as an autonomous spiritual activity. Largely derived, although we might hesitate to acknowledge it, from romanticism's claim that art is "the infinite made visible in finite, sensuous form," we look to art for the articulation in image, in form, of an intuition into self and world; we look for *aesthetic* power or force and for meanings that are intrinsic to the work; we look for structure and for formal relationships, as that which gives a spiritual character to art.

The emergence of art from religion is thus a process which continuously takes up, retains, and at the same time refashions the basic features in the early phases of their relationship. When art achieves autonomy, which to say, when *quality* becomes the primary category of art, aesthetic *force, meaning,* and *beauty,* as defined *sui generis* for art, become the inherent structure or aim of an artwork.

The power of an artwork, its "aesthetic force," is that elusive sense of life which, like magical power, is discerned to be in the work, but which, unlike magical power, is there as a perduring property: the force of an artwork is not dependent upon the work's being used in rite and ritual. "Aesthetic force," nevertheless, is "mysterious" insofar as it is inexplicable by reference to any set of quantifiable elements. The inner life of an artwork is not measurable: "aesthetic force" cannot be recorded on a scale; but it can be apprehended and indeed is apprehended whenever an artwork is experienced rightly as an artwork.

"Aesthetic force" may be defined, then, as the concentrated energy of the artwork; its *śakti* (to borrow an apt Sanskrit term), which shines forth and compels, as it were, a like-minded assimilation of it. Aesthetic force is the vibrancy, the drive, the vitality of the artwork; whether there subtly or blatantly, it is always there as a manifest presence. It is "magical power" become the immanent spiritual life and rhythm of the work.

Similarly with *meaning*. When art achieves autonomy its meaning is no longer to be found merely in a conventional set of symbols or in an independently formulated series of concepts; rather, its meaning is inherent in the work. The meaning of an artwork, in short, is its aesthetic content. The meaning is just what the individual work itself is in its presentational efficacy. The work may have a recognizable subject matter (although this is seldom the case with music or architecture), and the subject-matter (familiar images, representations, graphic symbols of whatever sort) may contribute to the work's meaning; but the meaning is not reducible to the associations that gather about the symbols or about the referential elements themselves. Indeed, artworks may be meaningful which dispense entirely with any explicit symbolic presentation.

When *quality* becomes the primary category of art, "meaning" in art becomes, then, a realization of the possibilities of the artwork itself. *A work of art is meaningful to the degree to which it realizes the possibilities which it itself gives rise to.*

The chief difficulty that one has in articulating the special inherent meaning of an artwork is to be found in our general theoretical dependence upon the notion that meaning = referentiality (in some sense or other); that "referential meaning" has primacy (if not exclusivity) for meaning in general. Leonard Meyer, for example, accepts a definition of meaning as " 'anything acquires meaning if it is connected with, or indicates, or refers to something beyond itself, so that its full nature points to and is revealed in that connection' " and concludes that

> Meaning is thus not a property of things. It cannot be located in the stimulus alone. The stimulus may have different meanings. To a geologist a large rock may indicate that at one time a glacier began to recede at a given spot; to a farmer the same rock may point to the necessity of having the field cleared for plowing; and to the sculptor the rock may indicate the possibility of artistic creation. A rock, a word, or motion in and of itself, merely as a stimulus, is meaningless.[8]

But a work of art is not a rock, or just a neutral stimulus. Works of art are precisely unlike natural objects in having their own meaning, in realizing their own possibilities independent of any particular mode of selective perception. A work of art may, of course, be perceived *extra-aesthetically*—by an art dealer as an object of potential profit, by a mover as something to be crated carefully and handled gently, and so on. Aesthetically, however, the work of art has (and is) an intrinsic meaning—its realization of the possibilities which it itself gives rise to.

"Meaning" in art is thus related more to axiological than to epistemic uses and/or senses of the term. It is closer to the sense of 'meaning' in the question, which is so often asked, "What is the meaning of life?" than in the question, "What is the meaning of 'God exists'?" When one asks about the meaning of life, one is asking about a "purpose," for something that, in the process of fulfilling, will provide one with a feeling of value or worth; one is not asking for the conceptual sense, or lack of it, of a proposition or pseudo-proposition. In the question of the meaning of life one assumes that meaning is a property (of life) and not a relationship (between a symbol and a referent). And so with art. The meaning of an artwork is the artwork itself as a process and a completion. But it is not a meaning in a void any more than the meaning of one's life, if it has one, is utterly self-contained or wrapped entirely within oneself. The meaning of one's life, as well as with a work of art, brings one into new relationships with the world; the realization of possibilities is always a *disclosure* as well as an inherence.

But what does it mean "to realize possibilities"? For a work of art, "realization," I would argue, means the *bringing of the work to an appropriate conclusion and exhibiting the process by which that conclusion is achieved.*

Works of art are *purposive* forms, which is to say that once initiated they strive to fulfill ends appropriate to them. Octavio Paz writes:

> The poem flows, marches. And that flowing is what gives it unity. Now, to flow not only means to move but to move toward something; the tension that inhabits words and hurtles them forward is a going to the encounter of something. Words seek a word that will give meaning to their march, stability to their mobility.[9]

And Susanne K. Langer notes, with respect to drama, that

Before a play has progressed by many lines, one is aware not only of vague conditions of life in general, but of a special situation. Like the distribution of figures on a chessboard, the combination of characters makes a strategic pattern. . . . Where in the real world we would witness some extraordinary act and gradually understand the circumstances that lie behind it, in the theatre we perceive an ominous situation and see that some far-reaching action must grow out of it. This creates the peculiar tension between the given present and its yet unrealized consequent, 'form in suspense,' the essential dramatic illusion.[10]

The poem, the play, as indeed the painting and the musical composition—whether the art be primarily one of "time" or "space" —creates its own conditions of expectation, prediction, and anticipation which call for resolution and fulfillment. Now, there are of course important differences to be noted in the "process of completion" among the temporal (e.g., music) and the nontemporal (e.g., painting) arts. In the former, the process by which an appropriate conclusion is achieved is rather directly noticeable—that is, the expectations and fulfillments are immediately exhibited as constituting the work; in the latter, a kind of indirect reconstruction is required. For both cases, however, "process of completion" means not only apprehending what is actually realized, directly or indirectly, but having a sense of the way in which the appropriate, informing selections are made. When experiencing a painting, then, or any other nontemporal artwork, one is called upon to see it, not only as a finished thing, as something static, but as a dynamic "resoluting" of various tensions and contrasts as they develop integrally in the work as it seeks its right fulfillment. And the progress toward fulfillment—the process which is exhibited—is not, of course, mechanical; it is not a matter of the artist setting down initial words, colors, lines, and spaces and then having everything else inevitably follow from this setting down, as conclusions might from premises in a deductive argument, for the "appropriateness" of a conclusion or consummation of the work depends as well on elements of novelty and surprise; or, to put it another way, appropriateness in a conclusion calls for originality, for new disclosures, related to thematic dimensions (e.g., the metaphor in a poem which reveals unexpected qualities of a thing or relationships between things) or to more purely formal considerations alone (the technical accomplishment or skill which opens new potentialities or extends old limitations of the medium).

The "own possibilities" which an artwork realizes thus calls for *integrity* in the medium—"integrity" as a 'wholeness' and as 'honest use' of material. A work of art defines itself not only in the sense of the artist's selection of elements, with initial selections influencing, but not determining, what consequently occurs, but also in the full affective sense of its establishing its own special and appropriate tone, its own unique and right articulation of feeling—the feeling which suffuses the work and gives unity to it. "To be true to the medium," to use the materials of a medium honestly, on the other hand, means to work *with,* as well as to extend control *over,* the inherent qualities of the material. The artist must be at once servant and master of his medium. With motion pictures, for example, *the* art form for millions today, the realization of possibilities with respect to the medium itself means that the film must be a film *of* (something or other), for that is its very character as film, as photographic image; and yet at the same time—in order that a *mindful* aesthetic distance can be established between viewer and film (one of the most difficult tasks for film which tends peculiarly but quite naturally to absorb the spectator in ways which make for a certain mindlessness)[11]—the film must exhibit an exploitation of itself as a medium. The successful film—as an art form—is that film which is at once transparent, leading the viewer to that which is filmed (the action per se), and opaque, calling attention to itself as a self-contained structure of formal elements. Most movies are entirely transparent and hence are readily exhausted. They are "entertainment" precisely because of their failure, in terms of the demands of art, to use the medium with full integrity. The film which is an artwork—and indeed there are a surprisingly large number of them—is one which has its own meaning in and as a *particular* structured whole that is at once transparent and self-sufficient.

A work of art, we have said, is a process and a completion. It is, when successful, a realization of a conclusion that is appropriate for itself and an exhibition of the achieving of that conclusion—which exhibition involves working with both given and self-created conditions. The dance critic John J. Martin writes:

> This is perhaps the cardinal consideration in the approach to dance composition, namely, that movement of whatever kind carries within itself the implications of mood, purpose, function, emotion.[12]

He also goes on to say that

> By the dancer's prevailing awareness of the space in which and through which he moves, he relates himself consciously and visibly to his environment, and not only to the physical aspects of that environment but also to its emotional overtones.[13]

And, we would add, the dance also creates its own space. There is the natural space of the actual, physical environment (a stage of a certain size) in which and through which the dancer moves; and there is the space that the dance itself defines, the space intrinsic to the dance.

In short, there are given and self-presented conditions in art, with the artwork having the power (of course through the artist) to determine itself within that matrix. Self-determination for artworks, as well as for persons, takes place within a context of "existential conditions" which call for fulfillment. The meaning of a work of art is thus an expression of the freedom of art to be itself. Freedom means precisely the power to realize the possibilities that a thing (a person or object) sets for itself. The most meaningful thing, ontologically, would be the freest thing, which at the same time would be the most creative/created thing—and that is clearly where the work of art has its being.

Art becomes autonomous, we have said, by virtue of its own *quality,* and it strives, when autonomous, to be at once aesthetically forceful, meaningful, and beautiful. We have so far discussed aesthetic force and inherent significance or meaning. Let us turn briefly to *beauty.* Beauty in art, we have come to believe, is not reducible to the "attractive," to the "pretty," or to what might answer to any simple formulas for "perfection"; beauty has to do with aesthetic authenticity, with what is right for the individual, particular work of art as an aesthetic presence. The beauty of the work thus becomes inseparable from its aesthetic force and meaningful content. It becomes the artwork itself as a radiant form.

'Radiance' and 'splendor' of form have a medieval-sounding air about them, with some recent modern movements (such as pop art or even abstract expressionism) seemingly denying the notions entirely; yet they remain indispensable for understanding the intentionality of art as an autonomous form of life and being—because art, by its nature, expresses a transcendental striving. What is formally right for an artwork is not a *given* in nature; it is a *creative achievement* and thus always points beyond itself to a depth or dimension of spiritual being. Art *as* art cannot help being beautiful; the abstract (or nonabstract) expressionist work, as well as a Cézanne, strives for a formal achievement that is right for it—and succeeds as a work of art insofar as it exhibits that achievement.

In sum: art may be said to emerge from religion, first from its identification with religion by way of its centering in magical or holy *power*, and second from its subservient role in communicating an independently formulated *meaning*. It becomes autonomous, then, by virtue of its own *quality* and strives, when autonomous, to be at once *aesthetically forceful, meaningful, and beautiful.* When art is autonomous it has its own *intentionality*.

II

The question 'What is art?' can be, and indeed has been, addressed at several different levels and kinds of generality. It may be dealt with as a problem in the "philosophy of art" and accordingly answered in overarching metaphysical terms (Hegelian-like: 'Art is a spiritual activity of man which is delivered from a sensuous medium and contains an end bound up with it'); or it may be dealt with somewhat more empirically, art being characterized by those features which supposedly set artworks apart from other objects or which appropriately elicit a special aesthetic experience.

But, it has often been recognized, there are linguistic and logical difficulties in the question itself which seem to rule out any fruitful answer to it. First of all it might be the case that what we accept as works of art is so extraordinarily rich and diverse, including as it does exquisite Chinese vases and mammoth Gothic cathedrals, simple songs and symphonies, lyric poems, abstract paintings, statues of gods and portraits of kings, that what is true about, or holds for, all objects in the class is very little indeed, and not very interesting. Further, the question seems always to have been asked (and answered) relative to the art of a particular cultural time and place. The very import of the question 'What is art?', in other words, is culturebound—and perhaps inescapably so. Also, the question appears to invite not so much a *description* or definition of what art is as a *prescription* of what art ought to be. Underlying the answer to the question is usually a call or a program for what the answerer believes art ought to be (e.g., as in Tolstoy's famous essay entitled "What Is Art?").

Following Wittgenstein, some aestheticians (notably Morris Weitz) have also argued that it is impossible to formulate a conception of art through articulating necessary and sufficient properties of artworks; it is logically impossible, they say, to define art by any set of essential features that distinguish artworks from everything else.

> The problem of the nature of art is like that of the nature of games, at least in these respects: If we actually look and see what it is that we call 'art,' we will also find no common properties—only strands of similarities. Knowing what art is is not apprehending some manifest or latent essence but being able to recognize, describe, and explain those things we call 'art' in virtue of these similarities.[14]

'Art', the argument goes, is an "open concept": that is, "its conditions of application are emendable and corrigible."

Maurice Mandelbaum, in his article "Family Resemblances and Generalization Concerning the Arts,"[15] has nicely criticized this view by pointing out that to claim "family resemblance" only (as defined by Wittgenstein) for works of art overlooks the fact that there is an attribute common to all who do bear a family resemblance, although it is not necessarily one among those characteristics that are directly exhibited—namely, common ancestry. Artworks may have "relational attributes'' of this sort—although it might indeed be extremely difficult to articulate them. Also the fact that the art world is not closed to new and different forms does not, as Weitz seemed to think, mean that 'art' is necessarily an ''open concept.'' Future instances to which the concept of art may apply can, of course, possess genuinely novel properties, but the instances may nevertheless still come under a properly formed definition or general concept of art.

The answer to 'What is art?,' Mandelbaum rightly insists, is not to be found by *turning away* from the question but by *looking deeper*.

When art, emerging from religion, achieves its own autonomy or integrity, artworks, as we have seen, aim to be at once powerful, meaningful, and beautiful. If this is what artworks themselves strive to achieve, then the problem of finding (or even looking for) essential and exhibited, defining properties of all artworks does not arise. A work of art is that concrete form which aims to be at once aesthetically forceful, significant, and beautiful. Aesthetic force, significance, and beauty become the ''deep structure,'' the fundamental intentionality of art. They become its primary categories or ''relational attributes.''

Let us look further.

art is "imitation"

The instinct of imitation is implanted in man from childhood, one difference between him and other animals being that he is the most imitative of living creatures; and through imitation he learns his earliest lessons; and no less universal is the pleasure felt in things imitated (Aristotle, *Poetics* 4.2).

The earliest philosophical theory in the West about art is that art is a kind of imitation (mimesis). Plato interpreted mimesis as ''copying'' —the artist was concerned, Plato argued, to represent sense-objects by a replication of their sensuous properties. Aristotle, on the other hand, who thought that imitation was an instinctive force in man, developed a somewhat more sophisticated use of mimesis and seemed to argue that art imitated primarily the typical or universal dimensions of actions, characters, or events, disclosing thereby their general significance. "What art imitates," writes W. D. Ross, "is 'characters and emotions and actions'—not the sensible world, but the world of man's mind. Of all the arts the least imitative, that which can least be charged with merely trying to duplicate something already existing, is music; but for Aristotle it is the *most* imitative." [16]

It was left for Plotinus, however, the more ardent follower of Plato, to reject explicitly Plato's restriction of imitation to the copying of sense-objects. Plotinus insisted that the soul can rise to the principle of Beauty and that Beauty, as well as other Ideas, can be reflected in the mind of man as eternal models for his creativity. The arts, Plotinus writes, "give no bare reproduction of the thing seen but go back to the Reason-Principles from which Nature itself derives, and, furthermore, that much of their work is all their own; they are holders of beauty and add where nature is lacking." [17]

The neoclassicism of the seventeenth century, however, which once again called for art to imitate nature, neglected the Plotinian interpretation in favor of the notion that imitation meant a rulebound following of the general structures of nature. *Verisimilitude* came to mean an imitation of ideal types. As applied to the human scene:

> . . . for a painter or poet, not actual men and actions with their baffling mixture of good and bad, but types of character and purified logicized fables leading in a way analogous to the syllogism to a consent of the mind, and to virtuous deeds, composed the true model in nature. [18]

After having been largely set aside under the impact of romanticism, "imitation" in recent times has again been seen by some scholars and critics to be a central concern of art. Leo Steinberg, for instance, has argued that "art through the ages shows unmistakably that most of it is dedicated precisely to the imitation of nature, to likeness-catching, to the portrayal of objects and situations—in short, to representation." Steinberg sets aside efforts to explain away this historical fact by those who interpret representation as "an adventitious element in art—a concession made to populace or church" or by those who insist that "modern art, by eschewing the outgoing reference, constitutes something radically different and new" in favor of holding that "modern art has not, after all, abandoned the imitation of nature, and that, in its most powerful expressions, representation is still an essential condition, not an expendable freight."[19]

Susanne K. Langer, however, has observed that

> It is natural enough, perhaps, for naive reflection to center first of all round the relationship between an image and its object; and equally natural to treat a picture, statue, or a graphic description as an imitation of reality. The surprising thing is that long after art theory has passed the naive stage, and every serious thinker realized that imitation was neither the aim nor the measure of artistic creation, the traffic of the image with its model kept its central place among philosophical problems of art. It has figured as the question of form and content, of interpretation, of idealization, of belief and make-believe, and of impression and expression. Yet the idea of copying nature is not even applicable to all the arts. What does a building copy? On what given object does one model a melody?[20]

But some works of art do primarily copy, or attempt to copy, external objects of sense; others to represent the essential character of a particular thing, person, or event; still others to present the universal or typical features of a class of things; and yet others perhaps to "imitate" in none of these ways. What sense of "imitation," then, is applicable to all successful artworks? How does "imitation" relate to, and help further to explicate, the intentionality of art to be aesthetically forceful, meaningful, and beautiful?

"In early Greece," Wladyslaw Tatarkiewicz observes, "*mimesis* signified imitation, but in the sense in which the term is applied to acting and not to copying."[21] Imitation in art, I want to argue, means properly an "acting out"—a drawing from the very root of spiritual being so that the artwork can present or *perform* with power its own aesthetic content or meaning. To imitate in art means properly to have the expressive content of the work grounded in reality. That work of art is most truly imitative which is a concentration of the power of spiritual being. To imitate in art thus means to be determined by reality at the most essential level of spirituality. It means to have one's creative drive be in accord with—be derived from—a spiritual rhythm and power of being.

To be "grounded in," to be "rooted," means to be "tied to," which means rightly to be "influenced by": in the fullest sense of 'influence,' it means to "partake of the essential character of" that which is the source of influence. "Imitation" is thus a property, not a relation; which is to say that it is a quality become inherent in the artwork rather than something that obtains between the artwork and some object or process external to it.

"Imitation," in this sense, thus helps us to understand the assertion that a work of art is its own meaning; that art is autonomous. The assertion does not properly argue (as Clive Bell has done) that art need not draw anything from life and that "to appreciate a work of art we need bring with us nothing but a sense of form and color and a knowledge of three-dimensional space";[22] nor does it argue that a work of art should (or should not) have a recognizable subject matter, that it should (or should not) represent something or other; it argues that the aesthetic content of the work, if it is to be meaningful, must, at its deepest level, bear the strength and confidence of its being influenced by one or more aspects or dimensions of reality. But how is that possible?

Schopenhauer, who although among the last of the 'rationalist-idealist' thinkers about art (with his claim that artworks were not only graded objectifications of a metaphysical will but embodiments, in varying degrees of lucidity, of the Platonic Ideas), argued forcefully that *imagination,* or the creative insight of "genius," was the most *objective* form of consciousness. In contrast to fantasy-makings, which satisfy only the wish-fulfilling needs of the ego, imaginative construction, he argued, when properly understood, is always imitative insofar as it discloses the essential character of reality, not as a symbol pointing to it, but as a direct presentation of it.[23]

"Imagination" can be defined as the bringing inward of a world perceived in the present through the creation of relationships between objects (or events) as structured by memory.

Contrary to popular opinion, imagination is not an act of withdrawal from actuality; it is precisely an intensification and exploration of relational experience, of one's involvement with an "other"—with some one or more aspects or dimensions of reality. Imagination takes one outside one's little ego-based world by bringing the world into oneself. Imagination is an opening of the mind to reality; it is an act of appropriating experience and, through the appropriation, of overcoming one's estrangement from it.

As noted by Schiller and others, imagination is a kind of *play:* it is a free creative activity. The creativity of nature, it is believed, is utterly bound to governing laws and principles (gravity) or to fortuitous happenings (random selection). Human creativity, on the other hand, is not "necessary." The process has causes and reasons and it has limits (and indeed the artist often feels a certain necessity in that special need which creative expression alone can satisfy), but, when genuine, the creativity is self-determining and thereby free. When I create a poem, a piece of music, a garden, I am playing: I am engaged in an act for its own sake. Although nature sets limits to my act (I cannot compose music in a range outside human aural perception), I am acting spontaneously, with discipline, from the center of my being. I am, therefore, acting freely.

Imagination means a freedom from the seeing of things in terms of habituated responses and a freedom to create an ordered work. Through imagination (which is always informed by intellect) one structures experience, one articulates new relationships between things, one gives order and value to what might otherwise be commonplace, but,—and this is the crucial point,—the imaginative act, by its very objective character, is bound to reality. Whenever imagination is free, it enjoys an obedience to reality, a being influenced by it, a partaking of its essential character.

And, at the same time, it has its own subjective nature which is also reality-oriented, for without memory there is no imagination. This doesn't mean that if one were to suffer amnesia one would be unable to engage in artistic creativity; it means that an intensification of one's past experience made evident to consciousness is necessary for creativity in art. Imagination works on the (outer) present through the (inward) past. It demands that one bring forth past intensities of experience, especially those which are rather useless for simply adapting to, or working in, the present, and that one unite them with a vividly perceived content. Imagination is thus always allied with insight or intuition and hence differs from mere "imaginings," with which it is often confounded, just in this way—with daydreaming or a mere play of memories there is only the past or a wish-fulfilling future; with imagination there is the structuring of the present through the intensities of the past. With daydreaming and the like, one is absorbed in oneself; with imagination one is out of oneself through the appropriation of the present and the bringing forth of something that is new. With daydreaming one involuntarily roams the gamut of one's desires; with imagination one concentrates consciousness only on those relations that are to be structured.[24]

Imagination or artistic intuition, however, unlike the more purely spiritual intuition associated, say, with philosophical mysticism, does not demand a complete transcendence of the self. It is more an absorption of the self, a self-forgetfulness, in the intensity of a concentrated act than it is an utter self-surrender or self-denial. Its "content" is always at once phenomenal and noumenal, as it were, involving as it does a sensuous media and a silent spirituality—a power or rhythm of being (*ch'i-yun,* or "spirit resonance," as the traditional Chinese called it). Imagination and creative insight in art does not take place independently of its expression, its embodiment in form. One does not have an artistic intuition into "spirit resonance" and then search around for a means of expressing it; rather, the seeing and the expressing are, and appear, as necessary to each other.

Creativity in art, in other words, has to do with working with a particular *medium.* (It is extraordinary how this is occasionally forgotten.) Imagination, creative insight, is carried out in and through the materials of the art form, and thus always involves intelligent or critical judgment. Recent analyses of creativity in art do take this into account, but then in their eagerness to rid themselves of any romantic vestiges, they err, it seems in the other direction; they understand creativity to be just the exercise of this critical control, and they lack thereby any sense of the struggle, of the triumph, of the terrible or the joyful in creativity.[25] These analyses also err in neglecting the profound sense that the master artist has that he is more a *locus* than a *source* of the power of his work, that he is the place where creative powers meet; in short, to use the old formulation, that he is an *instrument* of nature and not just a controller of a medium, that nature is working through him—that his creativity is a kind of imitation.[26]

Imitation in art is thus like the primitive magic of the art-religion work in its effort to "embody" a spiritual force, but it is unlike it in insisting that the force, the power, is for itself as it informs its own aesthetic content and not for control over—or otherwise establishing a relationship with—something external to it. Imitation is a drawing from and thus is a presentation of (not a copying of, a representing, a being a symbol of, a reflection of) the power and rhythm of spiritual being. "Imitation" enables an artwork to be its own meaning and indeed to achieve the appropriate radiance and splendor of form which we see as the distinctive quality of that work of art which is beautiful.

art is "expression"

Oil is "expressed" from the olive; juice from the grape. Traditional expression theories of art claim that an artist lets out his feelings and emotions in such a way that they are no longer simply turbulent, blind, and chaotic, "expression" being a kind of ordering and self-clarification; and that, as clarified, the emotions are then embodied in the work of art and cause or elicit an appropriate response or recognition in the experiencer of the work. To express, according to the theory, is thus different from merely "to arouse" or "to exhibit" raw emotion, mainly by virtue of the lucidity or intelligibility that is said to be achieved by both the artist and the contemplative participant. Speaking of the actor's art, R. G. Collingwood, for example, writes:

> . . . if his business is not amusement but art, the object at which he is aiming is not to produce a preconceived emotional effect on his audience but by means of a system of expressions, of language, composed partly of

gesture, to explore his own emotions: to discover emotions in himself of which he was unaware, and, by permitting the audience to witness the discovery, enable them to make a similar discovery about themselves. In that case it is not her ability to weep real tears that would mark her out a good actress; it is her ability to make it clear to herself and her audience what her tears are about.

This applies to every kind of art. The artist never rants. A person who writes or paints or the like in order to blow off steam, using the traditional materials of art as means of exhibiting the symptoms of emotion, may deserve praise as an exhibitionist, but loses for the moment all claim to the title of artist.[27]

Most expressionist theory of art, as John Hospers has pointed out,[28] is confined to analyzing the expression of emotions or feelings; little is said about the artist's expression of ideas and concepts (although Tolstoy tends to combine the two when talking about the artist expressing the Christian idea of brotherhood). It is also based primarily on a *causal model* of the relations that obtain between artist, artwork, and the experiencer of it. The model assumes that the artwork which results from the artist's expression of emotion is itself essentially a means to (cause of) a particular effect, namely, the experience of one who contemplates it.

But an artwork is an object of concentrated meaning and value. It is more a *source* than a cause; it is where aesthetic value is discerned. The feeling import of an artwork is in, or simply is, the artwork as much as any of its formal qualities. The artwork, we would argue, doesn't so much cause or evoke, or make for a simple recognition of, an emotion (of sadness, gaiety, or whatever); when properly responded to, it is recognized as having its own expressive power, meaning, and quality.

An artwork is the expression of power insofar as it presents a forceful aesthetic content, which manifests the artist's successful transmutation of raw creative power into a controlled feeling which suffuses the work. ''Imitation'' refers to the going to the root of aesthetic force in spiritual power, the grounding of creativity in reality; ''expression'' refers to the actual presentation of that force by the created work of art.

The artist and the artwork, in this dimension, are thus as one. Criti-

cisms of expression theory which want to leave the artist and his creativity completely out of the picture when judging a work of art (e.g.,
Hospers: "when we make a judgment of aesthetic value upon a work
of art, we are in no way judging the process . . ."[29]) go to another extreme to avoid the naïveté of the traditional theory, with its emphasis
on the subjective or personal emotions of the artist. The creative process is one thing, the critics say; the work of art is something entirely
different.

But it is surely the case that a work of art is what it is by virtue of a
particular creative process; that the being of an artwork is its own becoming, if these terms may be allowed. The artwork, in short, is the
process of its being: the brushwork is the painting or drawing as assuredly as is its final color disposition. The aesthetic force of the painting,
we might then say, is the power of its coming-into-being, a power
which is controlled and disciplined and is to be found, as it were,
everywhere in the work. Lacking that power, artworks may be pretty
and decorative, but they would fail to fulfill the intentionality of art
itself, which aims to be powerful, meaningful, and beautiful.

When a discrepancy is evident between an isolable content in art (a
conventional symbolic meaning, literal reference, or message) and a
sensuous form which adorns the message or meaning to ease its communication, we have either propaganda (disguised sociology, politics,
etc.) and/or simply bad art. In a genuine or successful artwork, "expression" *constitutes* the aesthetic and *irreducible* meaning of the
work; it doesn't convey a separate meaning—or symbol of emotion.

Following Susanne K. Langer, we can, I think, properly say that an
artwork is an *expressive form*—but only as it is *creative of the meaning
that is expressed*. Langer is surely correct, however, in noting that an
artwork

> . . . is a symbol in a somewhat special sense, because it performs some
> symbolic functions, but not all; especially it does not stand for some-
> thing else, nor refer to anything that exists apart from it. According to
> the usual definition of 'symbol,' a work of art should not be classed as a
> symbol at all. But that usual definition [of something standing for
> something else] overlooks the greatest intellectual value and, I think, the

prime office of symbols—their power of formulating experience, and presenting it objectively for contemplation, logical intuition, recognition, understanding.[30]

But what, then, is the import of that which essentially creates and is its own meaning? "Imitation," we have suggested, has primarily to do with the influence of reality on the artwork, the manner in which, through the objectivity of creative consciousness, the aesthetic content is informed by reality. "Expression," we now suggest, has to do with the manifest presence of formal relationships that constitute the work, relationships which, imbued with feeling, derive their significance from their own inherent rightness. This is, in a way, circular; but it is a circularity that is inevitable and is itself revealing of the uniqueness of meaning (a meaning that does not merely stand for something else, or that is merely associative, i.e., gathered about a particular subject matter) that is present in any successful work of art. It is the particular way in which an individual work of art presents itself as suffused with feeling in and through its own aesthetic content which makes it count as an expressive form.

Vincent Tomas believed that one of the virtues of the concept of "objective expression," which is defined as that which "has the capacity to cause, under assigned conditions, an aesthetically expressive effect in a contemplative perceiver of it,"[31] was that it enables us to see that "Not all *objectively* expressive objects are products of artistic expression. We may," he says, "adopt the attitude of aesthetic contemplation toward natural objects, such as sunsets, real landscapes, and driftwood; and, when we do, we find our experiences of them have their feeling import. Yet no one embodied his feelings in them."[32]

But 'adopting an attitude toward' something is not the same thing as 'apprehending the qualities of' that thing. "Expression" as related to beauty, we would argue, has precisely the virtue of enabling us to distinguish sharply between works of art and sunsets and pieces of driftwood—exciting and interesting as the latter might be.

An artwork, unlike a sunset or piece of driftwood, expresses beauty just as the expressive form that it is, which is to say, once again, that its process and its presence are inseparable. It is when we radically sunder artist from artwork and artwork from a contemplative participant who has adopted a certain aesthetic attitude of detachment that we fail to recognize the special intentionality of art to be powerful, meaningful, and beautiful, which intentionality, when fulfilled, is integral in the artwork. The aesthetic quality of an artwork, in short, is not an isolable *formal arrangement* any more than its meaning is an isolable symbolic content. The quality, the beauty, that is achieved and presented by the artwork is its formal rightness and, inseparably, its aesthetic force and significance. The sunset and the driftwood may offer interesting, aesthetically complex arrangements of formal qualities—of lines, colors, textures—and an aesthetically appreciative attitude toward these objects is no doubt desirable; but the discernment of these qualities is not the same thing as the experience of quality in art. The latter requires more than an attitude of detached attentiveness to abstracted formal qualities (one is *impressed* by a sunset, with something of the literal meaning of the term, as 'being passively affected by' it); to experience the quality of an artwork as it is an expressive form requires the full play of one's intellectual and intuitive as well as one's sensuous powers of discernment.

We have argued that to formulate a right conception of art we must not radically sunder the artist from the artwork and the artwork from the contemplative participant of it.[33] An artwork is what it is by virtue of a "creative process," which process (of intellect, feeling, intuition) enables an artwork to be at once imitative and expressive and to fulfill its intentionality to be aesthetically forceful, significant, and beautiful. At the same time the artwork has its being, as it were, in a world of consciousness (it *is* as an artwork rather than just as a physical thing only for consciousness), and hence as such it cannot be conceived as completely independent of the experience of it.

Aesthetic experience has often been reduced to, or analyzed exclusively in terms of, either an aesthetic attitude (of disinterestedness, detachment) or an aesthetic *emotion* (of intense pleasure). Since Kant, at least, it has become commonplace to oppose an aesthetic attitude to a practical one. An aesthetic attitude, it is said, is one which is for its own sake; the object of perception is not, as is the case with a practical attitude taken as a means to some further end, but is approached as it is an end in itself, worthy of our close attention. In aesthetic experience we must disengage any personal or utilitarian interests we might otherwise have in the object in favor of attending exclusively to its intrinsic qualities. We must, it is said, be detached so that we may be open to what is presented by the artwork. An appropriate "distance" must be interposed between ourselves and the artwork in order that we may experience the artwork aesthetically.[34]

Now, however the "aesthetic attitude" is to be defined, it is evident that this attitude (basically of our openness to the work) is not itself the essential character of aesthetic experience; rather, it is a *condition* for that experience. Before one can relate to an artwork (or to a natural object) as an aesthetic object one must suspend one's practical and other inhibiting interests in it. This suspension is necessary for the apprehension of the aesthetic qualities of the object, but it is surely not sufficient for our experiencing the work rightly in the fullness of its being. A proper "aesthetic attitude," in short, might enable us to experience an artwork properly, but the attitude assuredly is not the basic nature of the experience itself.

Clive Bell has argued that "All sensitive people agree that there is a peculiar emotion provoked by works of art" and that "We have no other means of recognizing a work of art than our feeling for it."[35] Now, whether this "aesthetic emotion" is ours as such or is "objectified" as pleasure in the artwork (Santayana), it is clear that this emotion is also not the essential character of our experience with artworks, for it does not take into account the special cognitive and spiritual dimensions of the experience; the "aesthetic emotion" is at best only a frequent accompaniment to the experience. When the experience of the artwork is under the control of the work, the full intentionality of the work must be disclosed.

The experience of an artwork (which is aesthetically forceful, significant, and beautiful) involves, I believe, *assimilation, recognition,* and *discernment* and calls for a special *appropriation* which yields an integrated wholeness. Let me explain.

In actual life when we meet a situation of power, of force (especially of violence), we react to it, we protect ourselves from it, we might even act forcefully in turn; with works of art, on the other hand, we assimilate the aesthetic force; we take it on, as it were, as a condition of our own being; we incorporate it into our emotional texture and freely accept it. Assimilation is a kind of empathetic embrace, but it is not an attributing of a psychophysiological process to a particular shape or configuration (Vernon Lee's "mountain rising"); it is rather an *awakening* of our feeling to what is presented by the artwork. It is our being influenced by the work, as the work, through the artist, was itself influenced by a power and rhythm of being.

The aesthetic force of an artwork, in short, is not—when the work is right—one that just overwhelms the experiencer of it; rather, although it might appear initially alien to him, it is presented as an opportunity for his relationship with it.

We *assimilate* aesthetic force. We *recognize* meaning. In aesthetic experience the inherent significance of the artwork presents itself to us as something to be recognized rather than as something to be known conceptually. Recognition is, of course, a kind of knowing; it has its own noetic character, but it differs from conceptual knowledge, discursive understanding, and abstract, rational thought by virtue of its immediacy and qualitative discrimination. To recognize means to *apprehend*: it means to see mentally that a work has realized possibilities that it itself has given rise to, that the work has been brought to an appropriate conclusion and is exhibiting the process by which that conclusion was achieved.

Recognition of this type presupposes, therefore, a keen sensitivity and a knowledgeable background. One is called upon to recognize novelty and originality and at the same time to take in thematic and other purely symbolic achievements, as well as affective tones; one is called upon, in short, to apprehend the full range of meaning that constitutes the work.

Meaning is the locus for the cognitive in art. In our experience of artworks we must be knowing participants. We are not called upon to know what the work "means" but to apprehend that meaning as it is the work.

We *assimilate* aesthetic force; we *recognize* inherent significance; we *discern* that the work of art is rightfully beautiful. Aesthetic experience, on its formal side, or in its formal dimension, is not just a noticing of qualities and a passing over the qualities to other aspects that interest one, as is the case generally with ordinary perception; it is precisely a close attentiveness to the play of colors, lines, shapes, sounds, spaces, and rhythms as they at once have their own integrity and contribute to the work as a formal gestalt. Discernment means discrimination and judgment; it is an *activity* of the experiencer; it is an active engagement between a work and the contemplative participant of it.

Now, assimilation, recognition, and discernment are not, in actuality, separate moments or features of experience; rather, they interfuse, intermingle, and together are the *process* of our relating to works of art. The process does require the full play of one's intellectual and intuitive as well as sensuous powers and, under the control of the artwork, may bring about an integration and wholeness to the experiencer of the work. And just as the creative process which brings the artwork into being is at the same time a self-articulation and self-formation of the artist, so this play of the experiencer's powers is a kind of self-appropriation—the realization of the self's own spirituality. Spirit meets spirit in art—and an integrated wholeness, however temporary or enduring, is achieved.

What religion earlier sought through a ritual use of, or amalgamation with, art is now attained by art in its own spiritual world.

In sum: art emerges from religion, first from its identification with religion by way of its centering in magical or holy power, and second from its subservient role in communicating an independently formulated meaning. It then becomes autonomous by virtue of its own quality and strives, when autonomous, to be at once aesthetically forceful, meaningful, and beautiful.

A work of art thus has its own intentionality, which is precisely its aiming to be aesthetically forceful, meaningful, and beautiful.

A work of art is aesthetically forceful to the degree to which it mani-

fests an immanent spiritual power, which power or rhythm of being is
everywhere present in the work and is discerned as its unique vitality.

A work of art is inherently significant, is meaningful, to the degree
to which it realizes the possibilities that it itself gives rise to; realization being a bringing of the work to a right conclusion and an exhibiting of the process by which the right conclusion is reached.

A work of art is beautiful to the degree to which it presents as its
own presence a formal achievement that is appropriate to it.

A work of art is imitative insofar as artistic creativity partakes of the
essential character of reality, with the work thus becoming a presentation of (not a copying of, a representing, a being a symbol of, a reflection of) the power of spiritual being.

A work of art is expressive insofar as it exhibits its creative process: it
is expressive of the vision of the artist, as that vision becomes the artwork's own aesthetic content.

A work of art is an object for consciousness and is experienced by assimilation (of its aesthetic force), recognition (of its inherent significance), and discernment (of its beauty); the three together form a single process of experience which culminates in a self-appropriation or
realization of the self's own spirituality.

A work of art is thus that created object which, when realizing its
own intentionality, is at once imitative and expressive and performs,
for consciousness, its own aesthetic content.

III

Thus, I argue that by "truth" in art we mean: *a work of art is true
when and only when it attains authenticity through the presentation
of its own intentionality.*

authenticity

A work of art is authentic when it has a dynamic completeness that is
natural and proper to it. Authenticity in art means the exhibiting of a
unique wholeness; the presenting of the object in and through its own

conditions of existence. A work of art, as we have seen, must always be in some medium (a poem must be in at least *a* language), with the medium imposing a variety of conditions on the work: a work of art, like a person, has its accidents of birth, its specific (historical) time and (cultural) place, with all the existential conditions (e.g., technical means available, cultural expectations and values) that these imply. A work of art that is authentic affirms itself by acknowledging these conditions.

But this acknowledgment means something more than the artwork's simply fulfilling or representing its conditions. An artwork that is only the fulfillment of its conditions becomes utterly clear, and thereby uninteresting; it becomes only an *example* that is explainable by its conditions (e.g., an inferior work of any particular "school"). Authenticity in art calls for creative uniqueness; which is to say that the dynamic completeness that is natural and proper to an artwork must always be irreplaceable. The artwork must acknowledge its conditions in the fullest sense of working with, but through, them to the realization of a special wholeness or integrity.

Integrity suggests strength and confidence. An integral X has no need of pretense, of masks. And artworks wear masks only unbecomingly. It is impossible "to fake" it in art, for although there may be fakes (forgeries) in art no work of art can survive the awareness that it is not really what it presents itself (pretends) to be. An artwork is an *exposed* being. It is highly vulnerable to a penetrating aesthetic consciousness. We readily, almost immediately, recognize the inauthentic—and reject it.

But when a work of art has integrity we accept the work for what it is. We affirm its being as being right for itself. "We expect a work of art to convince us," writes Dorothy Walsh, "but not by argument and not by evidence. Its authenticity must be internal to its concrete sensuous presence. Given this authenticity, we accept it. . . ."[36]

We are not likely to apprehend a work of art as true and at the same time to disvalue it aesthetically. For truth is not something that is superadded to (or subtractable from) the formal qualities of the work. Nevertheless, aesthetically there is more to an artwork than its truth, so that it does not follow that we necessarily ascribe "greatness" to a work that is true. (Truth in art is a necessary but not sufficient condition for aesthetic appreciation.) We may find the true artwork to lack an adequate depth of power, radiance, and meaning; but because of its integrity, its self-sufficiency, we advance mentally no alternatives to its presentation.

Now, a work of art has, of course, alternatives: in the sense of there being other possibilities for it entirely, there are an unlimited number, but when the work is true we recognize that it is right for itself, that it is *necessary* as it is. As Hofstadter notes:

> What is right, necessary, and an end in itself is what has attained to truth of being, i.e. to a condition of being in which it is as it ought to be in terms of its own ought.[37]

When we speak in formal terms of "necessity" in art, we do so it seems always in the context of our recognizing the work as a created object—one that is open to infinite possibilities, or to put it another way, one whose being is self-determined. In contrast to our experience of "design" in natural objects, where we recognize that the necessity governing the design is external, as it were, to it (the flower designwise is what it is—and nothing else—in terms of its being a particular expression or concentration of indifferent, universal forces and principles, it is a product of these forces), in our experience of artworks we discern (quite unconsciously and unthinkingly, no doubt) its freedom precisely as self-determination. Its rightness is *inherent;* it does not follow from natural laws but from the dynamic interactions of its elements as controlled by creative intelligence. The artwork is thus discerned by us in its full uniqueness as it is both itself and a world of meaning.

own intentionality

Judgments concerning rightness necessarily take place within a context of possibilities; within what I would like to call, following (while substantially revising) Hofstadter, an "intention."

> . . . in order that a thing should be objectively true, it must possess for itself the intention or concept which is in conformity with the thing's realized existence and it must realize this intention in its existence. The

thing must be one whose being, as a thing, is a realization of its *own* intention and whose *own* intention uncovers itself eventually as what it is. A true thing must be a self-attaining nisus toward a truth that is the truth of its own being.[38]

"Intention" is a difficult notion and one that is subject to a good deal of misunderstanding. To clear away one problem immediately: I do not mean that judgments about truth in art require us to know the intention of the artist (I doubt if it is ever—or at least it is very seldom—the case that an artist has a simple, identifiable, preconceived intention that is as such subsequently realized in the work; his intention, rather, is brought forth in the work during its making); I mean that any work of art intends its own mode of being; that it has its own essential character as a work of art, its drive to be the thing that is right for it.

The locus of intentionality, we want to argue, is the artwork itself; the intentionality of any thing is what the thing itself aims to be by its own nature, which aim, however, is not an abstract ideal (a projected model or externally imposed idea of perfection) nor a preexistent form (a latent idea or potentiality) of the thing, but that inherent power of the thing to give rise to the conditions under which its own authenticity is discerned. The intentionality of a thing is that drive of a thing to become what it ought to become according to its own process of development. An intentionality is thus an immanent objective of a being in-process. It is that which autochthonously sets the standard for itself as the kind of being that it is.

The term "intentionality" has come into prominence in contemporary philosophy through phenomenology. Following Franz Brentano who, in his *Psychologie vom empirischen Standpunkt* of 1874, distinguished "psychical phenomena" from "physical phenomena" according as the former has the characteristic of always referring to a content, as containing within itself an immanent objectlike entity, whether existing objectively or not, Husserl developed the idea of the intentionality of consciousness; that consciousness, by its nature, is always consciousness *of* an object. An intention is constituted *in* consciousness.[39]

Phenomenology thus uses "intentionality" as the characteristic way in which consciousness functions in relation to its world, the way, that is, in which mental acts present the subject with an object. We, on the other hand, do not restrict "intentionality" to human consciousness; for the immanent objectivity that we are concerned to identify (and hence our use of the term "intentionality") is, as we see it, a characteristic feature of entities like artworks and various language types, as indeed of human beings themselves.

"Intentionality," as we use the term, refers to that aiming for particularized expression that is part and parcel of the being of anything capable of realizing an intrinsic meaningfulness. The intentionality of a thing is not its "concept" (Hegel's *Begriff,* as Hofstadter seems to suggest); rather, it is the particularized concern of the thing to be what it ought to be, with the "ought" itself dynamically established in terms of the special circumstances of the individual thing.

Art, we have said before, intends to be aesthetically forceful, meaningful, and beautiful. The intention of a particular work of art, therefore, is precisely its drive to realize this general intentionality under the artwork's own existential conditions. A work of art, in other words, strives to be the *unique* thing that is right for it within the framework of the intentionality of art.

Archaïscher Torso Apollos
Wir kannten nicht sein unerhörtes Haupt,
darin die Augenäplef reiften. Aber
sein Torso glüht noch wie ein Kandelaber,
in dem sein Schauen, nur zurückgeschraubt,

sich hält und glänzt. Sonst könnte nicht
der Bug der Brust dich blendet, und im leisen
Drehen der Lended könnte nicht ein Lächeln
gehen zu jener Mitte, die die Zeugung trug.

Sonst stünde dieser Stein entstellt und kurz
unter der Schultern durchsichrigem Sturz
und flimmerte nicht so wie Raubtierfelle

und bräche nicht aus allen seinen Rändern
aud wein ein Stern: denn da ist keine Stelle,
die dich nicht sieht. Du musst dein Leben ändern.

Archaic Torso of Apollo

We did not know his legendary head,
in which the eyeballs ripened. But
his torso still glows like a candelabrum
in which his gaze, only turned low,

holds and gleams. Else could not the curve
of the breast blind you, nor in the slight turn
of the loins could a smile be running
to that middle, which carried procreation.

Else would this stone be standing maimed and short
under the shoulders' translucent plunge
nor flimmering like the fell of beasts of prey

nor breaking out of all its contours
like a star: for there is no place
that does not see you. You must change your life.

Translated by M. D. Herter Norton in *Translations from the Poetry of Rainer Maria Rilke* (New York: W. W. Norton & Co., 1938), p. 180.

Rilke's "Archaïscher Torso Apollos" is in conformity with its *realized* existence as just the poem that it is. It has its own essential character, its own drive to be right for itself, which rightness is brought forth and is "announced" only in the poem itself. Its vital meaning is apprehended only in itself, as it reveals itself to itself and to us. A work of art is always a surprise and a wonderment.

Paul Klee's *Heilige vom Innern licht,* to take an example from the "plastic" arts, is true. It is aesthetically forceful, significant, and beautiful just in its own way as a dynamic completeness that is natural and proper to it. It is a right presentation or articulation of its own intentionality.

Thematically one might ask: Who is the 'holy one' here? Where is he? Why is he holy? In the *Theologia Germanica,* an anonymous mystical work of the fourteenth century, we read:

Now the created soul of man has . . . two eyes. The one is the power of seeing into eternity, the other of seeing into time and the creatures, of perceiving how they differ from each other. . . . But these two eyes of the soul of man cannot perform their work at once; but if the soul shall see with the right eye into eternity, then the left eye must cease and refrain from all its working, and be as though it were dead.[40]

The soul of man, we are told, cannot at once see the eternal and the temporal, and consequently, it finds itself in tension. The "holy one" is the soul of man. And it is located at that precarious dividing line between the One and the many, between the divine and the world. It is holy precisely because it has the potentiality to see into eternity.

The soul of man, Klee is telling us, is a sea of infinite possibility. It can be involved completely in the world, or it can reach for the joy of a self-transcending contemplation.

Now, we may reject this metaphysics and assert, for example, that there is no "other world" at all, or that such a world can indeed be wholly immanent in our experience, but the truth of the artwork is not judged by this criterion. Truth in art does not require an assent to the world view or philosophy that might be suggested by or be "embodied" in the work. A work of art is not true *to* something else—its truth is not dependent upon its meaning being translated into propositions which correspond *with* or *to* some state of affairs external to it—rather, its truth, like its meaning, is inherent in it. Klee's work has integrity: its vision is articulated rightly with aesthetic force, meaning, and beauty—and that is enough. We may disagree with the world or human view suggested by it, but we cannot rightfully disagree with the work aesthetically because of its view.[41] We recognize aesthetically its authority and authenticity, its powerful manner of affirming itself. There is a masterful certainty in the line delineating the figure: the work does compel our like-mindedness. *Helige vom Innern licht* is authentic; but one would not also say that it is "perfect." Perfection in art (which often means just a static completeness) may in fact lead to falsity, to that which is entirely unnatural and inappropriate in the object that bears it.

Salvadore Dali's *Crucifixion* (originally entitled *Corpus hipercubus* or *Hypercubic Body* by the artist) has a kind of perfection, but it lacks integrity. Although Chester Dale, who donated the work to New York City's Metropolitan Museum of Art, claims that "it is a very honest picture, very great,''[42] one cannot but discern the disparity between the advertisinglike qualities of the painting, with its unsymbolic cross constructed of floating cubes, and its alleged symbolic values. There exists here an enormous gap between intention and pretension. The grandly robed figure at the lower left (said to be modeled by Dali's wife) is insipid (and quite dispensable). The work is an unchristian (and not even anti- or postchristian) Crucifixion, which is to say that it is inauthentic. The work does not achieve a dynamic wholeness through the acknowledgment of its existential conditions. The work does not appear self-affirming; it appears as highly artificial. It thus lacks integrity.

We contradict, we falsify, in art when we recognize that the artwork needs to be replaced in its own being with another possibility that would be right for it. We falsify (weakly) when we recognize unrealized potentiality; we falsify (strongly) when we recognize inauthentic realization; when, as with Dali's work, we recognize pretense, when we fail to find reality.

When the artwork is true, as with Klee's work, it has the aesthetic force, the inherent significance, the internal necessity, the rightness that exhibits strength and confidence and that calls for acceptance and assent to its being.

In discussing various criticisms of the traditional "coherence" theory of truth, Alan White writes:

> It is no objection to the truth of a statement in a particular mathematical system that there are or may be other systems with whose members it does not cohere. . . .[It] is logically possible to have two different but equally comprehensive sets of coherent statements. . . .[43]

What is logically possible for mathematics is, we might say, empirically necessary for art. One true work of art does not stand in competition with another work that is true. The truth of one work of art does not require the falsity of another work. The untrue in art is simply the unrealized and the inauthentic.

This brings us to one of the most difficult problems for the theme of truth in art—the matter of forgeries. There seems to be something very puzzling about a situation where an artwork is first experienced as a great work of art (or at least is regarded as great) by those considered to be best qualified to make the judgment (e.g., the Vermeer experts in relation to the famous Van Meergeren forgeries) and then without the artwork's undergoing any change in itself, upon learning that it is a forgery it is rejected and disvalued by the experts and by others who follow their judgments. We think somehow that the forgery ought still to be the cause of a satisfying experience if indeed it had that capability in the first place. We are ready to admit that its economic value might rightfully change, but we don't see how there can rightfully be a change in its aesthetic value.

The view of truth in art that I have tried to state can, I think, deal most effectively with this problem—for, in the simplest terms, the realization of an artwork's inauthenticity (in this case, the clear recognition of the disparity between the object as it is and as it, through another, claims to be) is precisely a basis for rejecting it. Our knowledge about what a thing is necessarily enters into our perception (interpretation, evaluation) of it. And when we appreciate the fact that the artwork *controls* experience and is not simply a *cause* of it, the problem of forgeries is dissolved. The forgery does not rightfully affirm its existential conditions (this is especially so when a contemporary artist manufactures a work for attribution to an artist of an entirely different period and cultural milieu), and hence it lacks truth. When controlled by the object aesthetic experience is always more than just a formalist response to (isolable) formal qualities; for the aesthetic force, significance and beauty of the work are inseparably present in the work as it is a structured content. We don't, in short, merely appreciate formal qualities of a certain kind apart from their having been produced in a particular way.[44]

We reject the forgery aesthetically, then, not because the work no longer conforms with (corresponds to) our idea of it (this would only trap us in that net of having the artwork be true to something external to it), but because the work is not true to itself. The forgery is inauthentic, and thus we are justified aesthetically in disvaluing it.[45]

And for the work that is true, as Alan White also notes:

A particular statement [or artwork] could be perfectly true without containing more than a minute proportion of the whole truth even about a single topic. Being wholly true is not the same as being the whole truth. . . .[46]

The true work of art is a wholeness, but assuredly it is not the whole truth. The art world consists of many presentations, some of which are right articulations of intentions which exhibit dynamic completeness. There are false works of art, and there are works of art that are true.

CHAPTER II
Truth in Religious Language

THREE TYPES of religious language need to be distinguished: "language *of*," "language *for*," and "language *about*."[1] Religious "language *of* " is the language of spiritual being. It is presentative and content-ful. Being the language of revelation, its truth is self-certifying. Religious "language *for*," on the other hand, is language which is to guide another to the realization of spiritual being. It is incitive and celebrative. Responding to it in a way which enables one to determine its truth calls for risk and commitment, for an act of "faith." Religious "language *about*" is the language of system and creed. It is interpretative and significant. It is also symbolic and formative of religious consciousness. Its truth is determined in terms of how well it communicates values and conditions consciousness.

I
religious "language of "

In what we have called religious "language *of*," the *what* and *how* of speaking are inseparable; which is to say, there is no "what" that can be separated from the manner, the "how," of its being said. To put it another way, in religious "language *of* " there is content but no subject matter—nothing that can be adequately translated or transposed into a set of independent statements or propositions. What, then, is the content of religious "language *of* "? It is, ontologically, the domain of silence: the very state of spiritual being. The content of religious "language *of* " is the spiritual rhythm and power of creative being. Religious "language *of* " is surcharged and suffused with an integrative vitality. It is thereby revelatory of spiritual being.

Now, it would be quite natural at this point to proffer an example of religious "language *of*," but I hesitate to do so for several reasons. First of all, it is simply not the case that all or even most persons are likely to agree that an alleged example is in fact an example of revelatory language. Any purported example must, of course, be in *a* language, and this fact already severely limits the opportunity for universal response (e.g., the familiar claim that the Qur'an loses so much of its spiritual efficacy when translated into other languages); religious "language *of*," unlike other forms of religious language, cannot be adequately "translated"; it can only be partially reconstructed. Second, the offering of examples might give the impression that the experience (and proper recognition) of religious "language *of*" does not call for any special qualifications by the experiencer at the time—and this would be a wrong impression. Just as it is most unlikely that in the course of an argument about the nature of poetic language one could simply hold up a poem, say by Dylan Thomas, and have the viewer experience that poem in its full poetic power, so to accept something as an example of religious "language *of*" calls for more than a simple recognition of a particular as belonging to a type; it calls for direct experience of, and involvement with, the unique, individual thing—and for that one must obviously be prepared. Religious "language *of*" is assuredly the rarest achievement, pointing to, as well as partaking of, as it does, the very depth of spiritual being.

All language, it is often suggested, is symbolic insofar as words, phrases, and sentences (whatever, in context, the primary language unit might be) "point to," "stand for," or "signify" things, relations, and meanings; but religious "language *of*" is symbolic in a special way; for it is at once wholly transparent, pointing to a divine presence, and entirely opaque, partaking of that presence in its own vital being. Most language use is "literal," is sign-language use which is translatable into many forms and expressions without there being a significant loss of meaning. An ordinary weather report can be given in a variety of (conventional) ways and languages and mean much the same thing. Most language as used simply "points to" and "stands for." Religious "language *of*" spiritual being, on the other hand, not only stands for but *is* its meaning. And it is therefore revelatory. When language is a world of meaning in its own expressed form it discloses an order of experience, a state of being, from, as it were, the inside out. It is not so much a matter of "pointing to" as it is "standing out from." Relevation means taking the standpoint of the state of being that is realized, rather than that of a subject confronting it. Religious "language *of*," the language of spiritual being, of revelation, is thus not *reduplicative* of reality, a representation of it; rather, it is *presentative* in its own right of spiritual being; presenting by its own vital fusion of "how" and "what," the natural-spiritual rhythm of being.

If, however, revelation is determined not by its subject matter but by the spiritual quality of its formed content, then in terms of religious "language *of*" religion may appear to be a mode of art. But revelation differs from a poem qua poem in that attention is called not so much to itself as to the divine presence which it shares. The poem controls our experience of it. Religious "language *of*" occasions our experience of the divine presence. But this, of course, does not preclude the possibility that artworks (and indeed other human makings and activities) may be revelatory of being. Revelation is not constrained to "religious language *of*"; it may be present whenever, with insight and love, divinity is made manifest.

The creation of religious "language *of*" which speaks from the plenitude of being calls, then, for an insight into silence and for a loving awareness of, a complete openness to, the infinite power and rhythm of being.[2] Word and meaning are made inseparable only through insight and love. But one cannot *intend* to be revelatory, to create religious "language *of*"; all intentions of this kind call for an activity that is to satisfy the intender, and where there is need there is necessarily separation and distance. Religious "language *of*," to be effectively communicated, requires for both the speaker and the hearer a self that is free as far as possible from desire and need. The word is spiritually efficacious only to he who is fully there as spirit to receive it.[3]

And this is what is meant essentially by "inspiration": utterance wherein the utterer, rather than being a self-conscious, isolated speaker, is an instrument for sacred sound. Sacred sound, religious "language *of*," the word wedded to silence speaks itself, as it were, from the very depth of one's spiritual being.

Truth in religious "language *of*" cannot, then, be a matter of correspondence between a statement and some state of affairs, between two different things open to public, objective inspection (as, it is usually thought, with assertions such as "It is now raining outside"); rather it must involve *discernment,* the *recognition* of spiritual quality. "Language *of,*" we must be mindful, is not *about* something. Revelation, as I understand it, is not a representation of some moral law or empirical fact; it has no subject matter: within the constraints of language as such it is simply the disclosing of the very life of spiritual being. Its truth, therefore, must be self-certifying, for there can be no other criterion drawn from other areas of experience which is appropriate to it. Religious "language *of* " is true when it rightly achieves its own aim to be revelatory. It is determined to be true when one recognizes precisely those intrinsic qualities of insight and power which constitute its meaning.

Religious "language *of,*" when recognized as true, has for us an authority which seems to demand our convincement (our openness to it, our orientation toward it, our acceptance of it). What makes language authoritative? First, when "language *of* " is authoritative for us we respond to an intense self-convincement on the part of the speaker. One is unlikely to be convinced in this area of experience by someone who is not himself convinced of his speech. Also, we respond to what we take to be an authentic basis for the speaker's self-convincement; that is to say, we discern integrity—that the "language *of* " is genuinely expressive of a realized, and not merely an imagined, state of being. Second, for "language *of* " to be authoritative for us it must seem to be commensurate with those possibilities of experience that we hold for ourselves. If the language is of a state of being that we cannot even imagine as possible to us, we will not find it authoritative; on the contrary, we will reject it; its alienability will be pronounced in such a way as to set up an insuperable barrier to our sympathetic assimilation of its content.

The recognition of spiritual quality, therefore, is the recognition of the truth of religious "language *of.*" And this recognition is, at the same time, the only possible test for its truth. When true, religious "language *of* " becomes authoritative for us. It reveals spiritual being.[4]

II
religious "language for"

As a fletcher makes straight his arrow, a wise man makes straight his trembling and unsteady thought, which is difficult to guard, difficult to hold back.

As a fish taken from his watery home and thrown on the dry ground, our thought trembles all over in order to escape the dominion of Mara, the tempter.

It is good to tame the mind, which is difficult to hold in and flighty, rushing wherever it lists; a tamed mind brings happiness.

The Dhammapada, chap. 3; trans. Max Müller

Be watchful and diligent in the service of God and often reflect: What have I come here for, and why have I left the world? Was it not that you might live for God and become a spiritual man?

Therefore be keen to make progress; for soon shall you receive the reward of your labours. And then shall there be neither fear nor sorrow within your borders.

A little while shall you labour now; and presently you shall find great rest, yes, everlasting joy.

Thomas à Kempis, *Of the Imitation of Christ,* chap. 25;
trans. Abbot Justin McCann

Religious "language *for,*" in its many and diverse forms (from the simple parables found in all religious traditions to the elaborate treatises of a St. John of the Cross or the vast Yoga literature in Hinduism and Buddhism), is primarily language that is intended to enable another to realize a spiritual state of being. Language is used here to point the way for another. Advisory, exhortative, celebrative utterance are intended, in this domain of religious discourse, to incite the hearer to follow some inner-outer path. Religious "language *for*" is necessarily interpersonal, and in an especially intense way. It is a *teaching* language. It doesn't so much reveal the reality of the divine to one who is prepared to receive it as it communicates with others the fruit of experience and addresses itself to the spirit seeking its way.

Religious "language *for,*" however, unlike most interpersonal speech, is not—when it is genuine—*to* the other (and thereby indicative of the need of the speaker more than of that of the hearer) as it is *for* him, in openness to his being. It also is thus grounded, when it is authentic or true, in a kind or nonegoism. It requires an attentiveness to the other, a sympathetic identification with him; at its best it requires in the speaker a bodhisattvalike freedom and compassion (*karuṇa*).[5]

Plotinus writes:

> [The truth is] 'Not to be told, not to be written': in our writing and telling we are but urging towards it: out of discussion we call to vision: to those desiring to see, we point the path: our teaching is of the road and the traveling: the seeing must be the very act of one that has made this choice.[6]

The "pointing" in religious "language *for*" is for those desiring to see; and here we have the special situation that the truth of the path depends as much upon the hearer—the one for whom it is intended— as it does upon the "what" and the "how" it is said. Truth in "language *for*" does, to be sure, involve a kind of "correspondence" between the signs employed and what is signified, between the map and the terrain to be covered (for the map must be "accurate"); but it also clearly involves pragmatic efficacy: religious "language *for*" is true to the degree to which it is efficacious for the one who is responding to it.[7]

And for the response to be efficacious the responder must begin with an act of "faith"; he must make the *commitment* to follow the path into what must still be for him dark and strange forests. He must take the *risk* of at least partial self-surrender to his guide. In short, he must be committed to the (correspondence) truth of the "language *for*" before he can in fact establish its truth pragmatically. It is only on the condition of faith (a kind of *credo ut intelligum*), and not from an outside, external attitude or position, that the truth of religious "language *for*," that the rightness of the teaching as given to one, can be determined.

Religious "language *for*" can thus only be *provisionally* true. Unlike with "language *of*," its truth is dependent on a variety of external conditions, and it is accordingly always open to falsification and to inadequacy if not to inaccuracy.

III
religious "language about"

Religious "language *about* " is the most familiar to philosophers and has posed the major problems for philosophy of religion. Religious "language *about*" is fundamentally intellective. It is "public" and "objective"; that is to say, it is language which appears to be reducible semantically to propositions and statements—to language-units whose truth or falsity can be agreed upon in principle by logical and empirical verifying procedures. "Language *about,*" unlike "language *of,*" always has a subject matter, something of which it is about. It is the language which we use to interpret experience conceptually; to draw out the implications of spiritual experience for other (noetic, ethical, aesthetic) areas of experience; and, when used in a theological and not just a philosophical context, to transmit a religious tradition, both in creedal and systemic terms.

Now, analyses of religious "language *about,*" whether concerned, as in the past, with its possibilities for expressing religious insights, or, as so often today, with its cognitive meaningfulness and logical status, disclose various inherent limitations of language in speaking directly about reality, about the life divine; and these limitations must be fully acknowledged. Nicolas Cusanus, for example, writes:

> From the self-evident fact that there is no gradation from infinite to finite, it is clear that the simple maximum is not to be found where we meet degrees of more and less; for such degrees are finite, whereas the simple maximum is necessarily infinite. . . .

> A finite intellect, therefore, cannot by means of comparison reach the absolute truth of things. Being by nature indivisible, truth excludes 'more' or 'less', so that nothing but truth itself can be the exact measure of truth.[8]

And, as we have seen in our discussion of "language *of,*" in the apprehension of this self-certifying truth, that finite needful intellect which would make any comparison between the divine and the world simply no longer is.

The further one is from the life of spiritual being, the more one is compelled, it seems, to talk about it. The closer one is to the divine, the less one is capable of even uttering a name. When one inwardly possesses some thing on state of being, one has no need to objectify it. The finite intellect, in the realm of the spirit, works only on absences.

All "language *about*" is grounded in distinctions. To name some thing, to describe some event, to explain some process all necessarily presuppose the existence of radical subject-object distinctions; for to speak meaningfully *about* anything requires a consciousness that intends objects. Words are themselves objects in this context and can stand only for other objects or objectified states. But for religious consciousness the divine is not an object among objects; it resists separation and overcomes all distinctions and can thus never be a proper referent of a language-about act—naming, describing, explaining.

"Language *about*" is timebound. One cannot speak comprehensively all at once; one can speak only word by word, heaping up meanings, to be sure, as one progresses gestaltwise toward structured patterns, but always in time. It takes time to think and speak. But the divine is timeless: although in some theistic views it is operative in history, the divine, nevertheless, in its own essential being, is said to defy all temporal categories. Hence no "language *about*" can adequately refer to it.

Similarly all language is grounded in spatial relationships. As Kant pointed out, we can think about something only in terms of a spatial (to him, Euclidean) category. Try to think of some *thing* that is nowhere. Our mind, our intellect, and therefore our "language *about*," are at home only in a spatially ordered world. But the divine is nowhere and everywhere—and consequently no "language *about*" can be adequate to it. And so on.

The awareness of these inherent limitations of language in enabling us to speak about spiritual being has, in recent times, been supplemented by positivist-analytic attacks on religious language, the claim being that this language is cognitively meaningless (under some form of a verifiability or falsifiability or confirmability principle).[9] And most efforts to establish the cognitive meaningfulness of religious "language *about*," when this language is taken to constitute assertions or propositions in a neutral-value context, have indeed proven rather fruitless. The challenge that Antony Flew, for example, put forward as a development of John Wisdom's argument in "Gods" to the effect that religious assertions are meaningless insofar as the assertor does not know what could count against them or will not acknowledge any conditions under which they might conceivably be falsified has not, it seems, been satisfactorily met. R. M. Hare argues that Flew misunderstood the nature of religious assertions, taking them as he did as if they were scientific hypotheses. They should be understood, Hare maintains, as *bliks*—as judgmental frames of reference, as basic life-orienting presuppositions. But by proceeding in this way (and in trivializing somewhat the basic import of religious assertions) Hare simply gives up on the truth-and-meaning question and removes religious language entirely from the cognitive domain.

Basil Mitchell, on the other hand, argues with Flew that the assertional quality of religious beliefs is indeed central to the belief but argues then that believers (namely, theologians) do indeed allow some things to count against their belief (e.g., apparently needless suffering counting against the idea of a loving God and giving rise to the "problem of evil"). Mitchell goes on, however, to insist that the true believer will not allow anything to count decisively against his belief—so we are back to "articles of faith," or disguised *bliks*. (See the discussion of this, and Flew's replies to his critics, in *New Essays in Philosophical Theology*).

John Hick perhaps goes the furthest, though, in fighting the battle on the ground set by the opponent. He also agrees that the assertional quality of "language *about*" is of primary importance and then attempts to show that religious statements, such as "God exists," can conceivably be verified in experience—with verification meaning for him "the exclusion of grounds for rational doubt." But the lengths to which Hick must go in setting up examples of possible post-mortem communions with Christ in "resurrected environments" suggest strongly that this is not the right way to proceed.[10]

Now these difficulties in establishing the cognitive meaningfulness, and thereby the possibility of the truth-claims, of religious "language *about*" have led many philosophical (namely, Protestant) theologians to look elsewhere for meaning and truth in religious "language *about*" and to find it in the symbolic values of religious discourse.[11] Paul Tillich, for example, has argued that "Man's ultimate concern [his faith] must be expressed symbolically, because symbolic language alone is able to express the ultimate."[12] And "The reason for this transformation of concepts into symbols is the character of ultimacy and the nature of faith. That which is the true ultimate transcends the realm of finite reality infinitely. Therefore, no finite reality can express it directly and properly."[13]

Tillich believes that a symbol shares with a sign in pointing beyond itself to something else but that unlike a sign, where the relationship between it and what is signified is entirely conventional, a symbol "participates" in that to which it points; it takes on, in itself, the qualities and powers of what it stands for. But here there are several problems; for this "participation" seems for Tillich still to be largely a matter of convention or custom and not a matter of the symbol's having the qualities and powers inherent in it—as is the case with "language *of,*" the only language which, it would seem, is properly symbolic in Tillich's sense. As he speaks of them, religious symbols, in spite of the alleged ultimacy of their referent, are culturebound; they are efficacious, he says, only for those who are able to link them to historico-holy or mythical events. Thus, although Tillich sees clearly that a religious symbol must participate in divinity (and has formulated this insight in a brilliant manner), in his way of treating them, especially by insisting that "they are responded to only within traditions," symbols still have the essential characteristics of signs.

Another rather obvious difficulty in this type of analysis is its tendency to confound symbols in religion ("father," "cross") with the symbolic dimension of religious language itself. Tillich, for example, as already pointed out, insists that "symbolic language alone is able to express the ultimate"; but he then goes on to treat symbols per se and the manner in which they combine in myths. The symbolic quality of religious language is then just interfused with symbols in language.

Further, when symbols are tied to cultural experience, it is difficult, if not impossible, to talk of their truth independently of that experience. Tillich says that some symbols are more capable "of expressing an ultimate concern in such a way that it creates reply, action, communication."[14] He also says that "the other criterion of truth of a symbol of faith is that it express the ultimate which is really ultimate."[15] From this he argues for the "superiority of Protestant Christianity."[16] If the truth of a symbol (of symbolic language) depends, however, in part at least, on its efficacy in calling forth response and communication, then one cannot argue for the superiority of one tradition over another, except maybe within a common, and thereby limited, cultural sphere. What sense could there possibly be in the judgment that the "cross" or the Passion is superior for a Hindu than to, say, his own Kṛṣṇa legends?

The capacity of the symbol to "open up dimensions and elements of reality which otherwise would remain unapproachable" must rest, then, not on its growing out of "the individual or collective unconscious," because then it could show only its dark side, as it were; but it must rest on a realization of spiritual being, which realization is independent of the language used to refer to it. Symbols in religion, which, it must be admitted, often obscure as well as reveal "elements of reality," are most fully efficacious only for those who are able to dispense with them. They function quite properly in religious "language *about*," in their partial efficacy, as a means of simplifying and clarifying complex and otherwise confused experience and of transmitting cultural views. They are adequate in this context, in the last analysis, to the degree to which they aid in promoting understanding of the nature and implications of spiritual experience.[17]

Another approach to the problem of the cognitive meaningfulness of religious language has been developed by both traditional and contemporary Catholic theologians in terms of a *doctrine of analogy*. Being somewhat more confident than Protestant theologians of man's ability to talk meaningfully about God, they have urged that "analogy is a mean between pure equivocation and univocation." (Cf. Cajetan [1468–1534], *De Nominum Analogia*.) Eric L. Mascall, a contemporary exponent of the doctrine, has argued forcefully that the doctrine is indeed efficacious when it combines the traditional *analogy of attribution* (where the predicate properly belongs to one of the analogates and only derivatively to the other; e.g., when Jones and his complexion are spoken of as 'healthy') with the *analogy of proportionality* (where the analogue is found in each analogate in the manner appropriate to their natures; e.g., 'life' as applied to cabbages, elephants, man, and God). "The conclusion," he states, "would thus seem to be that, in order to make the doctrine of analogy satisfactory, we must see the analogical relation between God and the world as combining in a tightly interlocked union both analogy of attribution and analogy of proportionality. Without analogy of proportionality it is very doubtful whether the attributes which we predicate of God can be ascribed to him in more than a virtual sense; without analogy of attribution it hardly seems possible to avoid agnosticism."[18]

Now, apart from other technical difficulties in the doctrine, difficulties which the theologians honestly faced, there remains the simple fact of incommensurability between the divine and the world (which is taken to be the primary "universe of discourse"), so that if the words used to talk about God—goodness, power, and so on—do not mean the same thing when they are used properly to refer to empirical beings and events, then—although they might be functionally meaningful in a variety of ways—they cannot by themselves be the basis for truth-statements about God. Once it is maintained that "the essence of God is as little known to us as is his life,"[19] then the conclusion rightfully drawn is that "If it were possible to make a statement about God that bore exclusively on the essential or conceptual order, that statement would collapse into sheer equivocity and agnosticism. . . ."[20] The doctrine of analogy, as Mascall then implicitly shows, is neither a means of articulating a positive knowledge about God nor a means of discovery of new knowledge about God; it is only a means of drawing out the implications of certain theistic *presuppositions*.

John E. Smith, in his recent work *The Analogy of Experience*, tries to build upon the traditional 'linguistic' approach to analogy, and at the same time to avoid some of its difficulties, by working from the notion of an *analogia experientiae*. Analogies, he argues, can be "valid means for rendering religious insight [*read* faith] intelligible"[21] when they are grounded in experience. Smith begins by arguing for the need for analogies somewhat along traditional lines:

> The resort to analogy in religious thought and discourse is dictated in the first instance by the obvious fact that while our experience of the world, ourselves and others is accessible and mediated through sensible things, no corresponding sensible apprehension of God is open to us.[22]

And, he also claims, no direct or intuitive apprehension is available either.

> Were a clear and direct insight into the meaning of the paradigm cases available to us, there would be no need to proceed by a circuitous route. But such an insight is not available and the entire biblical tradition testifies against its possibility for finite beings.[23]

Smith goes on to say, then, that

> The problem may be stated thus: if religious insight is to be made intelligible, and if such insight into the meaning of existence as a whole for finite beings cannot be a matter of immediate or intuitive apprehension, the question arises as to what feature of existence is able to perform the mediating function.[24]

And asserts that

> . . . human experience is the "proper part" in existence which has the capacity to represent and interpret the meaning of the religious ideas which in turn purport to express the meaning of existence from the religious point of view.[25]

Therefore:

> The proposal to employ experience as the basis for analogy in the religious sphere has two aspects: on the one hand, it means the appeal to specific experiences as a way of understanding religious concepts. On the other hand, it means an ontological claim concerning the status and function of experience as such, namely, that it is capable of serving as a medium of interpretation between the finite world and its ultimate ground.[26]

The problem, however, remains. For if, as Smith maintains, analogies of experience function on the basis of various similarities that obtain between the analogates, then it seems clear that one must experience both analogates before one can indeed note the similarities. It may certainly be allowed that one might experience one side only dimly (and therefore require the analogy for further elucidation); but to close off our understanding of the divine, except through the mediation of faith, on the basis of the impossibility of our having sense or intuitive experience of the divine, would, it seems, make any analogy itself unintelligible. Unless one could realize how 'God's love' is like and unlike our human love, no amount of telling one that it is similiar to, but different from, it will enable one to understand what is actually being said in the analogy.

We are brought, then, back to the point that analogies between the human and the divine do not so much function within the domain of religious "language *about*" as a way of attaining cognitive insight as they do within theological discourse which is concerned primarily to draw out the implications and presuppositions of a theistic faith. Forsaking his role and task as philosopher of religion, Smith allows that he is really concerned to show the intelligibility of the Christian faith; believing, as he does, that "In encountering Christ one encounters the divine self expressing himself through another. Christ stands as the language which creates a community of understanding and of love between human and divine."[27]

One of the most interesting questions, however, that is suggested by the analysis of symbols and analogies in religion (a question which arises from the fact, already alluded to, that writers on religious symbolism often fail to distinguish between symbols in religious language and the symbolic character of religious language) is: To what extent is religious "language *about*" as such symbolic? To what extent is it *expressive and formative of religious consciousness?*

Religious "language *about*," I want to argue, is expressive and creative of (and not just allegedly descriptive of, or reportive about) the relations between man and the divine. When one assents to religious "language *about*," as Cardinal Newman saw clearly some time ago, one is not assenting just "notionally," as though statements of religious belief come under a simple propositional attitude, but one is assenting "really"; one is recognizing and accepting their formative value for consciousness.

The more that language is reducible or transposable without loss of meaning to context-neutral propositions (as indeed is the case with much theological writing), the less it comes under the general category of religious language. No language, except in a very broad nominal way, is religious by virtue of its subject matter alone. One could write about the history of man's relations with the divine as a work in history or sociology, or psychology. Religious language is not the same thing as language about religion. Language is religious language precisely in terms of its capacity to engender a special depth and intensity of involvement with its content; it is religious by virtue of its call for commitment and expression. Religious "language *about*," then, conditions a peculiar state of consciousness as well as communicating a body of abstract ideas and concepts. Religious "language *about*," when uttered and responded to in the context of faith or of immediate religious experience, not only implies but embodies an entire perspective on, or vision of, reality. To speak *about* is to establish a relationship *with*. Language achieves here the formation of self in relation to its world; it contributes directly to the quality of relation the self creates and sustains with the divine. In expressing the nature of the self and its world and in orienting the mind toward reality, language is not something external to the self or mind; rather, it becomes the very stance of the mind or of consciousness itself.[28]

Thinking about reality, talking about the divine, is, in other words, a *projective* act of the mind; it is, at this level of being, the manner in which the mind engages reality. Spiritual being is not grasped by our thinking or talking about it; it is not in this way reduplicated in our consciousness; rather, in our thinking and talking about it, it becomes the locus of consciousness, the place where consciousness is *at*. And consciousness *becomes* where it is at. It takes on the structure of relationships that it projects—and is thereby formed.[29]

Now, "existentialist" theologians (e.g., Martin Buber, Rudolph

Bultmann) have recognized this "subjective" grounding to religious "language *about*" and have illuminated the close relationship that obtains between religious language and experience. Buber states: "Meaning is to be expressed in living action and suffering itself, in the unreduced immediacy of the moment."[30] And "Every religious utterance is a vain attempt to do justice to the meaning which has been attained."[31] Hence, "every genuine religious expression has an open or a hidden personal character, for it is spoken out of a concrete situation in which the person takes part as a person."[32]

Going back to Kierkegaard, who insists that "God is a subject, and therefore exists only for subjectivity in inwardness,"[33] and that "The truth is precisely the venture which chooses an objective uncertainty with the passion of the infinite,"[34] Rudolph Bultmann argues that all religious "language *about*" puts the speaker outside the truth.

> For to speak in scientific propositions, i.e., in universal truths, about God means nothing else than in propositions which have their precise meaning in that they are generally applicable, that they are detached from the concrete situation of the speaker. But exactly because the speaker does that, he puts himself outside the actual reality of his existence, therefore apart from God; and he speaks of something quite different from God.[35]

To talk about does, of course, imply a *separation from,* a standing outside of, the object of one's speech; and the existentialist emphasis on this, with the insistence that religious meaning can never be understood apart from the passional existential character of the speaker, was a needed counterbalance to the objectifying intellectualism of rationalism (and today of the positivist philosopher who would dissociate religious language from its existential context). But in this one-sided emphasis on the "subjective" (rather than the "objective") what tends to get lost is just that projective quality that characterizes thinking and talking *about*. Religious "language *about*" is understandable only in relational and formative terms, as symbolic of an appropriation-seeking activity (a striving to attain religious meanings and values), which activity goes to determine the nature of the consciousness of the seeker. Religious "language *about*," in other words, is not just a disguised report of the subject's state of mind, or something to be replaced by passionate commitments and leaps of faith; it is itself communicative of values and is formative of mind. It expresses and directs consciousness and, in expressing and directing it, gives shape to the relationship that obtains between the individual and the divine.

In appraising the truth-claims of religious "language *about*" one cannot rightfully, then, adopt a naïve rationalistic attitude which would impose an innocent distance between our critical intelligence and the religious statement and treat the statement as though its meaning were reducible to a context-free propositional form. Religious "language *about*," although it must abide by the canons of consistency (or noncontradiction) and coherency and the rules governing semantic values, does not rightly function as a series of isolable propositions whose truth or falsity can be determined apart from the context of the speech-act. And this context involves the tradition within which the utterance is functioning. The tradition need not be a strictly "religious" one (i.e., Christian, Judaic, Hindu, etc.); it can just as well be a metaphysical or theological one (theistic, monistic, polytheistic, etc.). The point is that religious "language *about*" does not stand on some kind of neutral metaphysical ground. It functions always in a wider context of belief and conceptual organization; and it cannot be judged for its truth or falsity entirely apart from that language-conditioning and belief-determining context.

This does not mean, however, that the whole question of the truth of religious "language *about*" is to be cast into a restless sea where each current or wave may take its own valid direction; "language *about*" is not relativistic in this fashion; it means only that the matter of determining the degree of truth in religious "language *about*" that may obtain in any given instance is not a mechanical determination, like reading a number from an instrument; it is a process which demands *sensitivity* to what is being said by the sayer in the language in which he speaks and from what presuppositions with what intentions in mind.

The truth of religious "language *about*" is thus less a matter of correspondence between statement and fact (although when the language is true it will conform with, or putting it more properly in its negative form, will not be in conflict with, reality) and more a matter of a right formation of consciousness. Consciousness is formed rightly when it is in harmony with reality. Consciousness is in harmony with reality when reality itself shines forth in it.

When understood in this way, religious "language *about*" is not, then, less meaningful than the strictly propositional; on the contrary, it can be seen to have a cognitive richness that goes considerably beyond most propositional language, for it may be creative of relationships (which open the way to further insights) and not just presentative of facts. Religious "language about" can, of course, be false or, better, "inadequate," insofar as it fails to function creatively; but when it is what it should be—what it itself intends to be—then indeed it may be meaningful and true.

I have argued that there are three types of religious language that need to be distinguished—"language *of*," "language *for*," and "language *about*"—and that each has its appropriate criterion for the truth of utterances within it. Religious "language *of* " is revelatory and self-certifying; it aims to be reality, to partake of divinity. It is true when it fulfills that aim, that intentionality, when it successfully unites the "what" and "how" of language and, in its own vital rhythm, is presentative of being. Religious "language *for,*" on the other hand, is incitive and aims to direct consciousness to reality. It intends to be a teaching language and is true only to the degree to which it succeeds in directing someone's consciousness to the reality that is being sought. Religious "language *about,*" in contrast to propositional or assertional language which refers strictly to the empirical order and which is concerned to convey facts or to report states of affairs, is, while communicative of religious meanings and values, fundamentally formative of consciousness. It aims to form consciousness in relation to reality and is true to the extent that consciousness is formed rightly.

This, then, is the meaning of "truth" in religious language: the language is true when it fulfills its intentionality; when it is what it ought to be, as revelatory; as directive of self to reality; as formative of consciousness in relation to reality. The test for truth in religious language involves the determination by someone (who, on the basis of his own experience and sensitivity, is qualified to make the determination) that the given religious language is right for itself and is, thus, not contradicted by experience.

CHAPTER III
Truth In Propositional Language

I

IT IS A COMMONPLACE that only the *meaningful* (sentence, utterance) can (convey a proposition which can) be true or false; and therefore it is necessary that we begin our inquiry into the nature of truth in propositional language with a somewhat fuller look at the nature of "meaning." We undertake this "looking," not with the expectation that we will resolve any of the many complex and difficult problems in the philosophy of language as such, but rather with the somewhat more modest hope that a few often-neglected aspects of "meaning," which have relevance for the problem of truth, can be articulated.

the locus of meaning

It is assuredly the case, as Wittgenstein insisted, that language doesn't mean apart from its use by persons in a rich variety of contexts. 'Meaning' has to do with what human beings mean by what they utter and say. But this does not imply that the locus of meaning is "speakers" as such and not "what is said"; rather, it implies that speakers are necessary for what is said to have meaning.[1]

Stephen R. Schiffer, who follows and modifies H. P. Grice's account of meaning—"To say that a speaker S meant something by X is to say that S intended the utterance of X to produce some effect in a hearer H by means of the recognition of this intention"[2]—argues for the logical priority of speaker-meaning over utterance-meaning on the grounds that

In the first place, X is a whole-utterance type which means, say, 'snow is white' only if people do, would, or could mean that snow is white by uttering X. Roughly speaking and with reservations, one knows what a whole-utterance type X means only if one knows what a person would normally or ordinarily mean by uttering X. In the second place, it is possible for a person to mean something by uttering X even though X has no meaning.[3]

In support of the second argument Schiffer offers an example of S communicating to an audience A that he is angry because of his uttering "grrr." "In such an event," Schiffer states, "S may intend A to recognize that 'grrr' resembles the sound dogs make when they are angry and to infer in part therefrom that S's intention in uttering 'grrr' was to inform A that S was angry."[4]

But one could just as well say, in the first place, that A knows what S means only if A knows what X would normally or ordinarily mean when uttered in various contexts. We don't have access to a speaker's meaning independent of what he says. We do experience what he says and find it meaningful (to whatever degree) or meaningless. In the second place, it doesn't establish anything to say that "it is possible for a person to mean something by uttering X even though X has no meaning," for it is agreed that X (or any utterance whatsover) by itself, that is to say apart from a speech-act context, doesn't have a simple meaning; but if X is to mean in virtue of S, then it is still X that bears the meaning.

The criteria for meaning can be sought, then, only in what is said— in the context of a speech-act. The illocutionary force of X (its asserting, warning, promising, expressing anger or wonder or pain . . . to follow Austin) is possible only in a community of language users.[5] A warning or an expression of anger can be what it is only in the rule-related structures wherein a respondent R can recognize the illocutionary force, or what kind of statement is being made, only, in part, in virtue of his knowing, if only implicitly, those structures.

Some time ago, in Aesthetics, William K. Wimsatt and Monroe C. Beardsley in a well-known article, "The Intentional Fallacy,"[6] argued that criticism (understanding and appreciation) of a poem (artwork) has nothing to do with what an author "intended" by his work but only with the work itself. "If the poet succeeded in doing it [realizing his intention] then the poem itself shows what he was trying to do." Wimsatt and Beardsley call the claim that before one can judge a poem adequately or know what it means one must first know the author's intention the "intentional fallacy." They attribute it to the influence of romanticism, with its emphasis on the psychology of the author rather than on the qualities of the aesthetic object.

Now, the intentional fallacy can itself be fallacious if taken in an extreme or isolated way to mean, as apparently it did for someone like Clive Bell, that "to appreciate a work of art [or to know what it means] we need bring with us nothing from life, no knowledge of its ideas and affairs, no familiarity with its emotions," for this—and Wimsatt and Beardsley point in that same direction—would artificially isolate the artwork from that life wherein it has its being and make it utterly self-contained. We do bring with us our knowledge of life, our ideas, and our emotions to whatever we experience, and we experience things like artworks, when we experience them properly, as they are within the creative process of the artist and the critical process of our own informed experience. The "meaning" of an artwork, we have argued, is evident only in the full context of its being a work of art, which is to say, only as it is the realization of its own possibilities as these are determined and made evident through the creative process.

Similarly with language. What is uttered is not normally an impulsive, unconnected (incoherent) outburst (of the sort that would belong to the "meaningless"); what is uttered is uttered as a speech-act by a speaker to achieve various ends; it belongs to that process, and its meaning is internal to it just insofar as the utterance may be in connection with other utterances in the language in which it is uttered, in virtue of syntactic as well as semantic relations.

In short, it is one thing (and a very important thing) to realize that X (an artwork, a linguistic expression) has the meaning it has because of the process by which it came into being and quite another thing to say that what S (the artist, the speaker) meant has logical priority over what X means or that it is the primary locus of meaning. Speakers can mean something by their utterances only if the expressions uttered become bearers of meaning.

rules

In his work *Speech Acts,* John R. Searle distinguishes between two types of rule, the "regulative" and the "constitutive," and argues that "the semantic structure of a language may be regarded as a conventional realization of a series of sets underlying constitutive rules, and that speech acts are acts characteristically performed by uttering expressions in accordance with these sets of constitutive rules."[7] Regulative rules, Searle states, "regulate antecedently or independently existing forms of behavior; for example, many rules of etiquette regulate inter-personal relationships which exist independently of the rules."[8] Regulative rules, therefore, are those which "characteristically take the form of or can be paraphrased in imperatives."[9] Constitutive rules, on the other hand, "do not merely regulate, they create or define new forms of behavior. The rules of football or chess, for example, do not merely regulate playing football or chess, but as it were they create the very possibility of playing such games."[10] Constitutive rules, in short, which come in systems, "provide the basis for specifications of behavior which could not be given in the absence of the rule."[11] In sum, regulative rules apply to an activity whose existence is independent of the rules—they regulate preexisting activities; constitutive rules, on the other hand, apply to activities whose existence is logically dependent upon the rules—they both regulate and constitute an activity. To make a promise, for example, as a meaningful linguistic (illocutionary) act implies the rule that one is obliged to at least intend to fulfill it: that rule is constitutive of what it means to promise something or other.

But if we were to ask "According to what kind of rules does an artist create an artwork?," we would realize immediately that a satisfactory account could not be given in terms of regulative rules (R-rules) and/ or constitutive rules (C-rules) alone. It is certainly the case that some R-rules might be operative (especially in governing the use of conventional symbolization; e.g., if you are representing the crucifixion, you use the cross, etc.) and, although it may be very difficult to define them, certain C-rules as well (e.g., what counts as "music" in contrast to mere "noise," organized or otherwise, might be various defining notions having to do with scale, rhythm, etc.); but it is also certainly the case that R-rules and C-rules do not adequately account for the kind of critical judgments the artist himself makes in the process of creating his work, nor for what is meant by X being an artwork. For this, I believe, we need a new sort of rule, one that I should like to call *autochthonous-rules.*

"Autochthonous-rules" (A-rules), unlike R-rules and C-rules, derive from the rule follower's own sense of "rightness" in unique, nonrepetitive contexts. A-rules have this very special quality: they arise simultaneously with their application. When in the process of advancing a still-to-be-completed work of art, the artist, whether poet or painter or musician, exercises a critical judgment, informed by his knowledge (of the anticipated consequences of doing X upon all other existing elements) and by his taste. His doing X, instead of Y or Z, is not just fortuitous. Although there might be elements of arbitrariness in creativity, the process is governed by a sense of "rightness" in the particular situation that prevails. A-rules are rules insofar as they do govern or inform a process of intelligent making or doing; they structure dispositions of elements according to various standards; but—and this is especially the case in modern, nonhistorical styles—they apply uniquely to particular dispositions of elements. R-rules and C-rules are present to a greater degree in "stylized" artworks (a Gothic cathedral is defined as such to a considerable extent according to certain specifiable architectural principles), but even here they are not adequate, for a work of art qua work of art is always uniquely itself. It is never replaceable as a work of art by another work of art.

R-rules and C-rules may exist prior to any exemplifications of them (the rules of etiquette or chess may obtain even if no one was interrelating, or ever did interrelate, in a civilized manner; or was playing, or ever did actually play, chess); but A-rules exist only as they are applied; they are brought forth in terms of the elements which they govern. Some might object, therefore, that A-rules are not "rules" at all, precisely because a necessary condition for something to be a rule is that it does exist as such prior to, and independent of, that to which it applies. A sense of rightness, it might be argued further, may be an important factor in determining how and when one does apply various genuine rules, but the sense of rightness is not itself a "rule." Now, this could become a mere word-squabble; but if it would be helpful to someone to substitute "A-sense" for "A-rule" in order to appreciate the role of an autochthonous sense of rightness in determining meaning, then he should of course do so. I prefer A-*rule* because it shares the general sense of 'rule' as that which governs or informs a process of intelligent making or doing. In any event, the autochthonous sense of rightness is spontaneous; but not in the sense that A-rules spring forth from a void, but in the sense that they reflect the artist's entire experience of what is appropriate in a particular utterance-situation. "Appropriatenesss ties A-rules to cultures and makes for varying degrees of continuity in artistic traditions. A-rules, we will argue, are necessary to understand the nature of all forms of meaning.

the nature of meaning

In his effort to revise Paul Grice's account of meaning, which was summarized earlier, Searle appropriates Austin's "illocutionary act" and argues that "Grice in effect defines meaning in terms of intending to perform a perlocutionary act, but saying something and meaning it is a matter of intending to perform an illocutionary, not necessarily a perlocutionary, act."[12] Searle then points out that one of the most extraordinary properties of human communication is that "If I am trying to tell someone something, then (assuming certain conditions are satisfied) as soon as he recognizes that I am trying to tell him something and exactly what it is I am trying to tell him, I have succeeded in telling it to him. Furthermore, unless he recognizes that I am trying to tell him something and what I am trying to tell him, I do not succeed in telling it to him. In the case of illocutionary acts we succeed in doing what we are trying to do by getting our audience to recognize what we are trying to do."[13] And we do this by means of our utterance.

Searle goes on to insist on the role of rules in determining meaning: "On the speaker's side, saying something and meaning it are closely connected with intending to produce certain effects on the hearer. On the hearer's side, understanding the speaker's utterance is closely connected with recognizing his intentions. In the case of literal utterances the bridge between the speaker's side and the hearer's side is provided by their common language. Here,'' Searle says, ''is how the bridge works'':

1. Understanding a sentence is knowing its meaning.

2. The meaning of a sentence is determined by rules, and those rules specify both conditions of utterances of the sentence and also what the sentence counts as.

3. Uttering a sentence and meaning it is a matter of (a) intending (i-I) to get the hearer to know (recognize, be aware of) that certain states of affairs specified by certain of the rules obtain, (b) intending to get the hearer to know (recognize, be aware of) these things by means of getting him to recognize i-I and (c) intending to get him to recognize i-I in virtue of his knowledge of the rules for the sentence uttered.

4. The sentence then provides a conventional means of achieving the intention to produce a certain illocutionary effect in the hearer. . . . [14]

I have quoted Searle at length because I shall want to follow him in his understanding that ''one's meaning something when one utters a sentence is more than just randomly related to what the sentence means in the language that one is speaking'';[15] and I shall want, accordingly, to shift once again the locus of meaning from the speaker per se to what is said and to look there for the primary intention of the utterance. The intention of an utterance is its locutionary-illocutionary force; the intention of an utterance is what the utterance, through the utterer, is aiming to be—and ''meaning'' involves the appropriate exhibition and recognition of that intention.

A certain combination of words constitutes a statement or expresses a proposition, then, only if it is recognizable as aiming to present facts.[16] A symbolic expression is recognized as such only when it exhibits its intention 'to lead consciousness to,'' 'to uncover,' or 'to reveal' aspects and dimensions of self and world that otherwise remain hidden and inarticulate. Symbols are not usually self-expressive forms, as are works of art; although symbols, to be sure, may function integrally in works of art. Also, symbols seldom, if ever, appear in isolation; they function rather in a "language" with other symbols, in a certain cultural context, and for the most part are "readable" adequately only by those in the culture. In all these types, "meaning" requires the recognition of the intention of the utterance—what the utterance, in virtue of a speaker, is aiming to be or trying to do: once an utterance is recognized for what it is, it is *ipso facto* meaningful at this highest level of generality.[17] And we recognize intention rightly in virtue of our familiarity with both (some of) the elements which constitute the utterance (colors, shapes, forms in a painting; senses and references of words; etc.) and (some of) the rules which govern these elements.[18] The respondent to, the experiencer of, an utterance must be appropriately sensitive to what is uttered, which requires that he be familiar with a rich diversity of elements and with regulative and constitutive as well as with other autochthonous rules.

A-rules we argue, function in all forms of meaningful utterance, in varying degrees, and not only in artworks. When S utters, "It is raining outside" (as a locutionary-illocutionary act—say, he is asserting a state of affairs to his son in the context of his instructing his son to put on a raincoat when he goes outside), he does not utter it as a "talking machine" might (in some "lifeless" tone); he gives stress to certain syllables and the like, and he invests his speech-act with a certain language style. One's style of speech is governed, to be sure, by various regulative and constitutive rules, but, as with artworks, these rules do not fully account for the governance that occurs. With speech styles there is always the matter of the speaker's sense of "rightness" as the utterance is made in a specific context. One of the most irritating things about having to repeat what one has said in situations where this is called for by others is precisely the implied negation of this stylistic or A-rule governance. We resent the notion that what was "right" in the saying of X at time-place$_1$ is simply transposable to a time-place$_2$ even in those cases where the time interval is very small and is at the same place. We resent the idea that as speakers we are "actors." Our speech-acts, we believe, are *unique* occurrences, even though much that we may say locutionarywise is, we believe, transposable and translatable.

It is the presence of A-rules which give utterances the quality of uniqueness and which enable language to reflect the "character" of a person. What X means is a function of S's sense of what is right for X as X takes on this sense of rightness. A-rules establish the *tone* of utterances, and this tone is very much a part of the illocutionary force and intention of utterances and therefore of their meaning.[19]

Speaker, utterance, and respondent obviously must work together not only for bare communication to be achieved but for meaning to be present. An utterance will exhibit its intention only if the utterer knows what he is doing (i.e., knows how to make meaningful utterances in some kind of language), and the intention will be recognized only by those who have adequate knowledge of the elements and the various rules which govern them.

In formal terms, then, as a general statement of the nature of meaning, we have:

S utters (makes, shows, presents) X and X means M if and only if X exhibits its intention I in such a way that a (rightly sensitive) respondent R would recognize I in virtue of his familiarity with (certain of) the elements of X and (certain of) the rules (regulative, constitutive, autochthonous) governing (the elements of) X.[20]

II
propositional language

John Austin asks: "When is a statement not a statement?" And answers: "When it is a formula in a calculus: when it is a performatory utterance: when it is a value-judgment: when it is a definition: when it is part of a work of fiction—there are many such suggested answers." He goes on to say that "It is a matter for decision how far we should continue to call such masquerades 'statements' at all, and how widely we should be prepared to extend the uses of 'true' and 'false' in 'different senses'."[21]

'Our decision,' which seems to be in accord with common usage, is to restrict what we mean by "propositional language" to those statements about experience that have the presentation of facts as their primary aim and function. Propositional language is primarily *assertional* in character: it seeks to express that something is the case—and it is thus distinguishable from all forms of "religious language." Unlike religious "language *about*," with which it is most closely allied, propositional language is not fundamentally "formative" in character; it is rather preeminently *synthetic,* which is to say, its primary function is precisely to tell that something is the case.

Propositional language is also, then, to be distinguished from a language class that we will call "instrumentals." By "instrumentals" we mean those language forms such as definitions, laws, commands, performatives, the "truth" of which is entirely a matter of their conforming to the rules of the language used, to the logical demands of the system in which they may function, and to the requirements of the communicative situations in which they are uttered. The truth of instrumentals is their least interesting quality, as their truth, their rightness, simply constitutes the condition of their being what they are. Their truth, in short, is utterly transparent.

All analytic statements, therefore, come under the category of instrumentals, as do all other forms, if there are any, of so-called necessary truths.

It is common among empiricist-oriented philosophers to distinguish those principles or laws, such as noncontradiction, to which all thought must conform (e.g., if we didn't obey the law of contradiction every statement would be compatible with the affirmation of any other proposition), or, more generally, in terms made familiar by Quine, those "logical truths"—"A statement which is true and remains true under all reinterpretations of its components other than logical particles"[22]—from those statements whose necessary truth derives from the definitions of the terms occurring in it. Analytic statements of this second class or type (e.g., the paradigmatic "All bachelors are unmarried") are said to record our agreement to use words in certain ways. They do not really assert anything, as they cannot be either confirmed or infirmed by any fact of experience.

Now, it is not necessary for us to explain here the necessity of what is necessarily true; it is enough for us to point out that, in keeping with the nature of necessary truths, we exclude that class of language usage from propositional language. Propositional language, by definition, is empirically assertional. "Either p or not-p," "All bachelors are unmarried" do not intend to present facts. Analyticity, therefore, applies not to propositions, as we use the term, but to certain kinds of sentences.

A proposition, however, we can agree with Alan White, is "what is conveyed by a sentence."[23] Propositions are not mysterious "meaning entities" that hover over utterances; rather, propositions are embedded in language; they have meanings, to be sure, but meaning, as we have seen, cannot be identified with what language by itself allegedly says, as if the intention of the speaker and the particular language he uses, in his own style, were of no account whatsoever in determining meaning, and thereby the truth and falsity of propositions. We would agree with the sentiment expressed by Dorothy Walsh that

> The shift of attention from 'what language says' to 'what persons say,' that is the total speech act in its social setting, has had the salutary effect of shaking loose from the traditional philosophical preoccupation, amounting to obsession, with the assertive claim expressing a proposition true or false. It now becomes evident that, by the use of the declarative sentence, a speaker is not necessarily claiming: he may, for example, be announcing, which is not exactly the same. For the matter of that he may be describing or commending or disparaging or suggesting or threatening or warning. Also, he may be doing more than one of these by means of the same linguistic utterance.[24]

But when he is primarily asserting that something is the case, even when he is doing more than this, we have propositional language; language which assuredly has its meaning only in the context of the total speech-act but which aims to present facts.

In keeping with our analysis of religious language, we may then outline a typology of language—a typology which is intended not as an exhaustive organization of types of language usage (types such as "ethical discourse," while readily accommodated, are not specifically included) but as a schema for isolating propositional language in relation to religious language and to various "instrumentals"—as in the accompanying diagram.

TYPOLOGY OF LANGUAGE

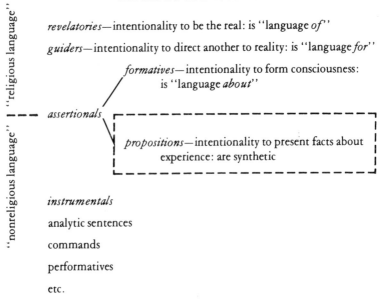

"religious language"

revelatories—intentionality to be the real: is "language *of*"

guiders—intentionality to direct another to reality: is "language *for*"

     formatives—intentionality to form consciousness:
        is "language *about*"

– – – *assertionals*

      propositions—intentionality to present facts about
         experience: are synthetic

"nonreligious language"

instrumentals

analytic sentences

commands

performatives

etc.

We restrict propositional language, then, to that language which is used primarily in an assertional way with reference to experience. Our position is that the *intentionality of propositional language is precisely that of presenting a fact.* A proposition is that which aims to present a fact.

facts

". . . What on earth could statements express except facts?" asks Moritz Schlick.[25] And, provided we may substitute "(meaningful) propositions present" for "statements express," we would agree that the answer must be nothing at all.

What is a fact? Etymologically the word is associated with the Latin *factum*, meaning "that which is done," a "deed," "act," "achievement," with this sense surviving only in various legal usages such as "before the fact" and "after the fact." This sense, however, is still influential in the manner in which "fact" is often confounded with "state of affairs."

A *fact,* we argue, *is a report of the occurrence or the nature of any content of consciousness.* We use the expression "content of consciousness" rather than "experienceable thing" because that of which facts are reports includes mental happenings as well as events and objects in the "external world." My thinking about unicorns can be a content as "objective" as the existence of a stone insofar as it is that which a fact may report about. By bringing events and objects in the "external world" into the category of contents of consciousness, on the other hand, we are not in the least concerned to argue for a "subjective idealism"—it is not a question of the being (the *esse*) of an event as a perception that interests us, but that the event or state of affairs can be characterized factualitywise in terms of its being a content of consciousness—we are concerned only to indicate that propositional language has as its domain anything of which we can be aware.

(True) propositions, we argue, present facts. And facts report states of affairs. A fact does not have a structure which "corresponds" to or with a state of affairs; rather, facts *tell of* the occurrence or nature of states of affairs. The fact *'that p'* brings to consciousness the way something is to us in our experience. Reporting is a kind or *awakening to* what is the case. In its full communicative context, reporting is a bringing of consciousness *to* some possible content *of* consciousness.

facts and states of affairs

This suggests that a sharp distinction must indeed be made between a fact and a state of affairs. A fact is that something occurred or is occurring or is the case. A state of affairs is the occurrence itself. It may be a fact that it is raining now; but a fact (notwithstanding the expression "cold, hard facts") is not cold or wet; rain is. Facts cannot be predicted; events (sometimes) can. We state or assert, we present, facts; we perceive, imagine, encounter states of affairs.

Facts, it is often pointed out, are atemporal, while events or states of affairs are timebound. "Facts, unlike states of affairs," writes Alan White, "do not begin, last or end. . . ."[26] "The battle of Waterloo," writes David Mitchell, "is an event in British history: that a battle was fought at Waterloo is a fact. The battle occurred nearly a century and a

half ago. It is over and done with. But it *is* a fact that the battle occurred at that time. Thus events have their places in time but facts do
not.''[27]

A fact *reports* rather that simply *describes* a state of affairs. ''Descriptions'' may indeed be assimilated to facts; but, except in those
cases, if there are any, where a name might denote an event with all of
its observable qualities, facts cannot be collapsed into descriptions.
''The gentle, soft rain refreshingly clears the air'' can be converted
factwise to ''It is the case that the gentle, soft rain. . . .'' But from ''It
is raining now'' you don't get a qualitative description of the rain.

If you want to know what a state of affairs p is, you look to the state
of affairs itself (as you are able to experience it). If you want to know
whether a proposition is true or not you look to see if it successfully
presents the fact *that p.*

By insisting upon a sharp distinction between fact and state of affairs we are not, however, leading ourselves into upholding a ''correspondence'' theory of truth. On the contrary, we believe that an ontological theory of truth applied to propositional language is able at
once to make sense out of propositional truth-claims (the nature and
test of truth) and to avoid nicely the many difficulties that have per-
sisted in classical and contemporary correspondence theories.

Aristotle is usually credited with having first articulated a correspondence theory in a manner that is still acceptable to many epistemologists. He wrote:

> To say of what is that it is not, or what is not that is it, is false; while to
> say of what is that it is, and of what is not that it is not, is true.[28]

This correspondence sense of truth, as we have noted earlier, came to
be formulated in the medieval period as *veritas est adequatio rei et intellectus*—''truth is the adequation of things and the intellect''; and
this sense has continued to serve as the basis for much recent discussion
about truth.

It was under the influence of Bertrand Russell, though, who was determined to counter the claims of the Idealists with their ''coherence''
theory of truth, that renewed efforts have been made to elaborate an

appropriate correspondence theory. In an early version of his theory Russell argued that

> When an act of believing occurs, there is a complex, in which 'believing' is the uniting relation, and subject and objects are arranged in a certain order by the 'sense' of the relation of believing.[29]

And that consequently

> A belief is *true* when it *corresponds* to a certain associated complex, and false when it does not.[30]

Most philosophers feel that there is something so undeniably right about the correspondence conception of truth that all that is called for is an adequate (and probably less complicated than Russell's) explication of it. Roderick Chisholm, for example, is able to say:

> Our question [What is truth?] is easy to answer if we allow ourselves a certain metaphysical assumption. . . . The assumption is that *states of affairs* may be said to exist or not to exist and that every belief and assertion (with certain exceptions to be noted) is a belief or assertion, with respect to some state of affairs, that that state of affairs exists.[31]

"What is truth?" has nevertheless, once the metaphysical assumption, at this level of experience, has been granted, proven to be a difficult question. The main problem for a correspondence theory has been to make sense out of what it means for a proposition "to correspond" to a state of affairs. Does correspondence mean "to copy" or "to resemble" or "to be structurally similar to" or "to be correlated with," and so on? What do negative propositions or hypothetical statements correspond to—in any of these senses?

Correspondence theorists have also found it difficult to explicate what it is that a proposition or belief may be said to correspond *to* or *with*. If, as seems to be the case with some structuralist interpretations of "correspondence" (e.g., that of H. B. Acton), it requires an unmediated state of affairs to which propositions correspond, then there is the clear objection that all of our experience is mediated by judgments and interpretations, and hence, under these conditions, "correspondence" would seem to be driven back to some kind of "coherence" conception; for the very meaning of correspondence, let alone the test for it, would be a matter of comparing one judgment with another judgment, not with an unmediated state of affairs.

By defining the "state of affairs" which facts report about as any possible content of consciousness whatever, we avoid the question of the *existence* of states of affairs, unmediated or otherwise. A state of affairs for an ontological theory of truth is any possible content of consciousness. It can be an "existing" object, like a tree; or an image, like a unicorn; or it can be an event, a happening, or a memory. And our propositions need not correspond with or to these contents so much as they must satisfactorily report about their occurrence or their nonoccurrence or their nature. *To report* does not mean *to correspond:* it means "to present" or "to announce" or "to point to." Facts do not report states of affairs rightly or wrongly (propositions present facts in this way); a fact is either a fact, or what appears to be a fact is something else; a fact, as a fact, reports a state of affairs.

One interesting and rather curious attempt to avoid some of the problems associated with the classical and contemporary formulations of the correspondence theory of truth is that put forward by the logician Alfred Tarski as a "semantic conception of truth." Tarski argues that truth must be understood as a semantic property of a *sentence*. It is the sentence, he insists, that designates what is in fact the case. Developing his theory against the background of the famous Liar paradox,[32] Tarski distinguishes between an "object-language" (the language that is talked about: "the definition of truth which we are seeking applies to the sentences of this language") and the "meta-language" (the language that is used to talk about the object-language: the language "in terms of which we . . . construct the definition of truth for the first [object] language").[33] Tarski points out that a sentence can be true or false only as it is part of some particular language. Those sentences which assert that a sentence S is true or false in some object-language L must belong to the meta-language in which the sentences of L are employed.

Tarski thus argues: "if the definition of truth is to conform to our conception, it must imply the following equivalence":

The sentence "snow is white" is true if, and only if, snow is white.[34]

He goes on: "Let me point out that the phrase *'snow is white'* occurs on the left side of this equivalence in quotation marks, and on the right without quotation marks. On the right side we have the sentence itself, and on the left the name of the sentence."[35] From this he generalizes and maintains that a definition of truth which is (materially) adequate is one from which all equivalences that have the form *X is true if, and only if, p* follow, with X being the name of the sentence and p the sentence whose name is X.[36]

But what this clearly leads to is a restricting of "true" to artificial or formalized languages. The rigorous semantic definition of truth which Tarski seeks (and he acknowledges this gladly) can have a precise meaning only in a language whose structure is exactly specified—that is, one in which "the class of those words and expressions which can be considered meaningful" can be characterized unambiguously.

> At the present time the only languages with a specified structure are the formalized languages of various systems of deductive logic. . . .[37]

A definition of truth which enables us to avoid self-referring generated paradoxes like that of the Liar must then be reached in the metalanguage and, for Tarski, employing a recursive procedure for defining "satisfaction"; such a definition is: "A sentence is true if and only if it is satisfied by all objects." In his concluding "Polemical Remarks" Tarski then adds:

> I do not have the slightest intention to contribute in any way to those endless, often violent discussions on the subject "What is the right conception of truth?" I must confess I do not understand what is at stake in such disputes.[38]

And I must confess I don't see what *philosophical* advance is made on Aristotle by a semantic conception of truth which finds "true" only to be a metalinguistic property applicable to *sentences,* and which only brings out, although in a rigorous way, the tautological character of the classical correspondence theory.

propositions and facts

An ontological theory of truth must hold that propositions are true when and only when they articulate adequately their intentionality to present facts. This does not call for a naïve "picture theory" where ideas or images represent reality in the mind. To present a fact is not literally to mirror the world; it is to communicate a report of a state of affairs.

Further, an ontological theory does not do injury to the fundamental commonsense intuition that a proposition is true only if there are entities and events in virtue of which it is true. The theory simply characterizes these entities and events in terms of their being possible contents of consciousness, with facts being reports of them. A true proposition and a fact must thus be distinguished—and an ontological theory is able to make the distinction more readily than a correspondence theory.

A true proposition, we have said, presents a fact. F. P. Ramsey, however, believed that common-language usage establishes an equivalence in meaning between them, for we interchange "It is true that" and "It is a fact that" without any difficulty. Ramsey then concluded that the adverbial phrases when attached to some sentence or other add nothing to what the sentence says on its own and that consequently "there is really no separate problem of truth but merely a linguistic muddle."[39]

But, as Alan White points out:

> It is not equivalence in meaning. For 'It is true that p' means 'It is true *to say* that p,' whereas 'It is a fact that p' does not mean the nonsensical 'It is a fact *to say* that p'; nor is 'The statement S is a true statement' equivalent to 'The statement S is a fact'. True statements, unlike events, can be long-winded, incomprehensible, badly expressed, in English, plausible, etc.; while facts, unlike true statements, can be stubborn, inescapable, or awkward.[40]

P. F. Strawson, on the other hand, has argued that Ramsey's "redundancy" theory is essentially correct but inadequate (while Tarski's semantic theory, he says, is wrong but important). Strawson criticizes the semantic theory that to say that a statement is true is to make a statement about a sentence of a given language on the grounds that a translator would not deal with a truth-claim as if it were a description of a sentence.

> For example, someone says, in French, "Il pleuve"; and someone else corrects him, saying: " 'Il pleuve' is *incorrect* French. 'Il pleut' is the right way of saying it." Or, criticizing the style of a passage, someone says: "The sentence '. . . .' is badly expressed." . . . In all these cases, it is natural to say that one is talking *about a sentence*. If any statement of this kind were correctly translated into any language at all, the sentence which was being discussed would re-appear, quoted and untranslated, in the translation of the statement as a whole. Otherwise the translation would be incorrect. But it is perfectly obvious that a correct translation of any statement containing the phrase 'is true' (used as it is ordinarily used) never contains a quoted and untranslated sentence to which the phrase 'is true' was *applied* in the original sentence.[41]

Strawson then goes on to argue for a *performative* conception of truth. "True" and "false" are not metalinguistic predicates or descriptive expressions; rather, they are used by us to agree and disagree, to concede and disallow, what has been said. To say that a statement is true adds nothing to the statement, but it is *to perform an action* of assenting to the statement.

> . . . in using such expressions, we are confirming, underwriting, admitting, agreeing with, what somebody has said;
> . . . we are not making any assertion additional to theirs. . . .[42]

But Austin, the "inventor" of performatives, while rather half-heartedly arguing for a correspondence view (halfheartedly because "the theory is a series of truisms")[43] rightly points out the inadequacies of Strawson's position. Austin writes:

> To say that I believe you "is" on occasion to accept your statement; but it is also to make an assertion, which is not made by the strictly performative utterance "I accept your statement." It is common for quite ordinary statements to have a performative "aspect"; to say that you are a cuckold may be to insult you, but it is also and at the same time to make a statement which is true or false.[44]

A proposition is true when it presents a fact—when it fulfills its aim and is the thing it ought to be. Facts are not what true propositions are or what they just state. A true proposition presents a fact. A fact reports a state of affairs.

articulation of intentionality

In order to present a report about a state of affairs; in order, that is, to present a fact, a proposition must be an *articulation* of its intentionality. A proposition must *mean* something; it must have a meaning; and it must, therefore, be conveyed by, be articulated in, a symbol system.

> A proposition is a particular thought that a speaker seeks to convey to his hearers, it is a meaning in the sense that it is what he, the speaker, means. Different speakers at different times and in different circumstances may use the same sentence to express different propositions.[45]

If in a theater I shout "Fire!," in addition to shouting a warning I am asserting, in a shorthand way, 'that there is a fire in the theater'; I am articulating the intentionality to present the fact that there is a fire in the theater. The single-word sentence, if you will, "Fire!," may, however, be inappropriately uttered in other contexts; for example, if in answer to the question "What is the most popular song in the country today?" I were to say "Fire": the proposition 'The name of the most popular song in the country today is "fire" ' is false: it doesn't fulfill its aim to present a fact.

> We could say that a proposition is true when it means a fact and false when it does not mean a fact. But the meaning of a word or of a combination of words cannot be determined by examining the nature of the words. Words have meaning only in relation to a mind that uses them to symbolize something. Hence what is true or false primarily is not the proposition as a verbal symbol, but what the proposition means.[46]

Meaning, we have already tried to show, is determinable only in communicative contexts. No sentence, or even just some combination of words, is inherently meaningless, as one can always imagine a communicative context with a set of rules for a code-language in which the most profusely category-mistaken-laden sentence can have a perfectly clear meaning. The code-language, in short, could function without any special difficulties in certain communicative contexts.[47]

Most philosophers have, however, tended to treat propositions, if not sentences, as if they had an independent, autonomous linguistic existence; but propositions, like sentences, are asserted by human beings to one another in various situations by various means, direct and indirect, for various purposes. Just as recent research in linguistics has shown "that modes of grammar have to take account of what Chomsky [in his transformational grammar] had arbitrarily ruled out," namely "the fact that language is used by human beings to communicate in a social context,"[48] so the long-standing tradition in philosophy to neglect the communicative dimensions of propositional language in favor of abstract or purely formal relations must be corrected to take account of that fact.[49] And as Austin noted:

> There are various degrees and dimensions of success in making statements. The statements fit the facts always more or less loosely, in different ways on different occasions for different interests and purposes.[50]

A true proposition is one that, to the degree and dimension appropriate for the occasion, successfully presents a fact; which is to say, one that rightly articulates its own intentionality so that it calls for response, reaction, and verification by those to whom it is conveyed. Whatever is correct in the *pragmatic* theory of truth is here accommodated in an ontological theory. We measure the utility value, as it were, of a proposition in terms of the degree to which it rightly articulates its own intentionality. Truth does *happen* to an idea, as William James was so fond of saying, insofar as an idea is an articulated form; insofar as it is a communicable meaning. But this does not mean that truth is "verification," that it is a time-dependent property of an idea, belief, or proposition that turns out to resolve a "problematic situation" (Dewey).

A proposition, to be true, we have said, must be an articulation, and it is important to realize that the articulation is not something that is done to, or is added to, a proposition; the articulation is rather the proposition itself in its presentative being. The proposition as a meaning, with its truth-quality there to be recognized, is only as it is articulated in some language.

And thus the proposition must necessarily be such that it "coheres" with the syntactical and semantical rules and usages of the language in which it is an articulation.

The *coherence* theory of truth which was developed from Hegelian Idealism, however, was based on a special understanding of the nature of thought and the relation of thought to reality. The aim of (rational) thought, it was believed, is to secure systematic completeness. "Thought in its very nature," writes Brand Blanshard, "is the attempt to bring something unknown or imperfectly known into a subsystem of knowledge, and thus also into the larger system that forms the world of accepted beliefs."[51] This is possible, according to the coherence theory, because of the manner in which, in reality, things are related to one another. Thought is essentially relational in character, and everything is said to be *internally* related to everything else.

The doctrine of internal relations in the coherence theory of truth is, as it is often pointed out, of central importance.[52] It is not clear what exactly is meant by an "internal relation," but a general formulation might be that X is internally related to Y when *any* difference in Y would mean a difference of some kind, no matter how slight or imperceptible, in X. Truth in thought would be obtained when ideally thought has become all the relations which go to form reality. Thought would then be identical with reality. "Fully coherent knowledge," writes Blanshard again, "would be knowledge in which every judgment entailed, and was entailed by, the rest of the system."[53] Now, it is admitted that this is the ideal, not the actuality, of our rational knowledge. "The system we actually work with is always more or less than *the* whole. . . ." "For all the ordinary purposes of life, coherence does not mean coherence with some inaccessible absolute, but with the system of present knowledge."[54]

Even with this concession, the difficulties in the coherence theory, especially as the *meaning* of truth, remain. Its uninhibited rationalism which sees truth only one-dimensionally as a nonleveled whole; its psychology of thought, which sees philosophic thinking only as discursive or dialectical and therefore as essentially quantitative and not qualitative; its inherent conservatism (the new must always be accommodated to the old); and obsession with system, which rules out spontaneity and radical change, is unacceptable.[55] But what is surely right about the notion of coherence in relation to truth is just the simple need for a proposition to be an articulation in such a way that it indeed makes sense to someone within a language. In any system of knowledge the proposition must cohere with other propositions, with various logical assumptions and principles, with various linguistic rules and conventions. Propositions are not isolated linguistic or atomic logical entities; for their meaning is as it is determinable both in a communicative context and within a logico-linguistic structure. Any proposition must be within the matrix of what makes a proposition a proposition, and this means its conformity to (its ability to be interpreted and translated according to) the rules of a language system.

true propositions

The intentionality of a proposition, we have argued, is to present a fact. A proposition is true, then, when it articulates its intentionality to present a fact. A proposition is false when it fails so to articulate its intentionality.

It no doubt sounds odd to speak of a proposition achieving a kind of ontological rightness. But when once we appreciate the importance of communicative contexts in establishing meaning and the ''pragmatic'' and ''coherence'' requirements of articulation, it ought to make clear enough sense how we can speak intelligibly about the rightness, or lack of it, of a proposition. A proposition, we have seen, is as a proposition only in articulated form. A false proposition would be a sham proposition: it would be one that failed to articulate its own intentionality to present a fact. It would not be what it ought to be according to the ought of what a proposition is or aims to be. The true proposition, on the other hand, would be one that is or has a meaning as an articulation that reports a state of affairs. It would be what a proposition ought to be. It would be a fulfillment of its own aim to be itself.

Now, fulfillment of aim, we realize, is most often relative; that is to say, an aim is more or less achieved. We have, then, this interesting characteristic of truth in propositional language: *a proposition is true or false* (the logician is paid his due respect), *and* there are degrees of truth-realization. A proposition either presents a fact or it doesn't. *And* propositions present facts with varying degrees of success.

III
the test for truth

We falsify definitively when we recognize that a proposition does not present a fact; that it has, in principle, a right alternative to it; we recognize truth as authentic being, we confirm or verify a proposition, only to greater or less degree, with better or worse sensitivities, in different contexts for specific purposes and interests. The test for truth in propositional language is that of our perceiving the rightness of a proposition, its fulfilling its aim to present a fact, in terms of our seeing whether the proposition has a correct alternative to it.

A proposition is seen by someone to be true when he recognizes rightness in such a way that there is no correct alternative to the proposition within the matrix of its presentation.

We contradict a proposition, we falsify, not by our replacing the proposition by some other kind of language type—for example, a definition or command—but by our rejecting it within the framework of the conditions and intentionality of the proposition itself; which is to say, in principle by another proposition that would be right for it.

For example, in a suitable language, A asserts that it is raining outside. B understands the meaning of the proposition—its presentation of the fact that it is raining outside—and recognizes that indeed the alleged fact does report a state of affairs, that it brings his consciousness to the rain as a state of affairs, with their being nothing in that bringing that contradicts the truth-claim of the proposition. B does not so much confirm without possibility of error that it is raining as he finds that he need not replace the proposition with another one that would be right for it. C, on the other hand, in the same circumstances, asserts to D that it is snowing outside. D likewise grasps the meaning—understands the sentence that conveys the proposition—but then recognizes that the proposition does not present a fact, as it is rightly replaceable by the proposition "It is raining outside." The former proposition does not bring a state of affairs to consciousness; the latter does. The recognition that a proposition does not present a fact, does not articulate its intentionality, is the recognition that there is at least in principle another proposition that would, in this context, rightly present the desired fact. In B's case, where the proposition is true, there is the recognition of rightness, the presentation of a fact.

With the true propositon, however, it should be noted, definitive *verification* has not taken place; there is an absence of falsification, of contradiction, and there is the realization of a measure of authenticity. With the false proposition, there is falsification; the replacement in principle of the proposition by another proposition that would be right for it.

Now, in some instances, and depending considerably upon the context, the simple negation of an "existential" assertion might adequately constitute a correct alternative to it. If someone were to assert, "There is a picture on that wall" when in actuality there isn't one, one would adequately falsify the proposition by a simple "There is no picture on that wall." In most instances and contexts, however, a simple negation is not adequate as a correct alternative, especially with propositions which ascribe properties to a subject. If someone says, "The sky is gray today" when in actuality it is clear blue, it is not enough to have "The sky is not gray today": falsification would call for "The sky is blue today."

The test for truth in propositional language is thus not one of noting a correspondence between a proposition and a state of affairs but one of noncontradictoriness. The proposition is formally true (is on the other side of falsity) when there is no correct alternative to it. There would be a correct alternative to the proposition as articulated if it failed to present a fact; if it failed to direct consciousness to a state of affairs. The test for truth in propositional language, in other words, is a determination of rightness that the proposition is not false; that there is no correct alternative to it within the matrix of its presentation. And all propositions, we would argue, are corrigible in principle. While facts may be incorrigible,[56] any proposition may conceivably fail to present a fact. A true proposition is uncontradicted; it is not uncontradictable.[57]

The degree of truth of a proposition, the degree of its rightness is a matter of positive recognition; for noncontradictoriness by itself does not provide us with a qualitatively differentiated perception. But these are not two radically different processes (logically or temporally); for rightness is recognized the moment that it is determined that the proposition has no correct alternative and is right for itself. In other words, we don't first see that a proposition is not-false and *then* say, "Ah! It is true!"; rather, the seeing is integral and one. When we see that a proposition does not have a correct alternative, we are at the same time seeing that it fulfills its own aim to articulate the intentionality to present a fact, and with all our sensitivities appropriately at play at the same time we recognize the qualitative degree to which rightness is realized.

CHAPTER IV
Truth as Rightness

WE HAVE REACHED the point now where, in the most general terms, we can ask: What is the meaning of "truth" that is appropriate to art, to religious and propositional language, and that may apply, *mutatis mutandis,* to any other candidate for being a bearer of the quality (e.g., a theory)? The answer, I believe, is that truth is rightness. In sum:

X is true when and only when it achieves rightness through the articulation of its own intentionality. X is perceived by Y to be true when Y recognizes that there is no correct alternative to X within the matrix of its presentation.

where

X is anything that has the capacity to realize rightness and *Y is a person qualified to perceive that X is true.*

I

Both traditional (correspondence, coherence, and pragmatist) and contemporary (semantic, redundancy, and performative) theories of truth essentially confine "truth," as we have noted, to propositions, statements, judgments, sentences, or beliefs—that is, to a restricted class of linguistic or mental entities.[1] Now, it should be noticed at the outset that "truth as rightness" is applicable to a very wide range of objects. As we have stated explicity, it is applicable to anything that has the capacity to be what is right for itself according to its own aim or intentionality. With the appropriate metaphysical assumptions one might thus allow for truth to be applied to (to be seen as a quality of) anything whatever. But it is quite evident that we are not ordinarily inclined to ascribe truth to so-called inanimate objects, like rocks and doors; for, in the first place, our perception of such entities simply is not usually carried out in truth-value terms; we do not assume that they have the kind of opportunity for self-control, for the freedom, if you will, to realize any state other than what they simply are. We are inclined to ascribe truth only to those things about which we can meaningfully say that they have (or are capable of assuming) an aim or intentionality. The range of applicability of "truth as rightness" that is of interest to us is where the truth or falsity of the thing makes a difference to us and to the thing.

To have 'the capacity to realize an aim or intentionality,' however, is not, of course, to be taken literally in the sense that the object (say, artwork or proposition) is assumed to have a volitional capacity just as human beings have. The intentionality of an artwork or a proposition is clearly imparted to it by human beings. But still there is very real sense in our speaking as if these objects had the capacity to realize their intentionality in a primary way, for one of the most interesting things about certain human makings, like artworks, is their tendency to have a life of their own; which is to say that once in process they go autogenetically to influence their own development, and in turn to contribute to the development of the maker of them.

It becomes clear, then, that "truth as rightness" rests on certain ontological assumptions; and these assumptions should be made explicit. The level of experience where rightness pertains is the level of our ordinary sense-mental experience. It is the world which we experience, in varying degrees, as ego-centered; it is the world as constituted by *particularity*. Rightness is possible only for particular things. Now, the ontological status of particularity might properly be called into question, especially when particularity is taken as an ultimate category, an incorrigible fact of existence; but it remains as a fact that the vast majority of the experience of most persons is carried out in a world which for them is made up of events, objects, things that are space/time-bound, that are in process, and that are interpreted and valued relative to their own needs, interests, and capacities. That to which rightness applies—the entire domain of what has the capacity to achieve authentic being—may be illusion *(māyā);* but that domain is nevertheless the stuff of experience and must, philosophically, be accounted for and understood as far as possible in its own terms.

Another way of putting the matter would be to say that if we want "truth" to mean just the way the world is, the way reality is in and of itself, then this 'truth,' which is obviously inaccessible to philosophy as such, is necessarily incommensurable with the application of the term to individual objects. This is the case because truth as pure being, as the way reality is, whatever that may in actuality be, would have to be "absolute," which is only to say here that one could not posit anything that could intelligibly contradict it. If reality is "truth," then, like Spinoza's "substance," it would be utterly self-sufficient. Nothing can stand outside 'all-that-is-as-it-is' to deny or negate it. The truth as pure being—or the truth of being[2]—would thus be peremptory, if not perennial.

Also, the apprehension of truth as being would call for the realization of the perfect coincidence between appearance and reality. It would mean the presentation to consciousness of being as it is. Now, this apprehension, if it were possible, would clearly require a dramatic shift from our ordinary sense-mental experience to some other mode of consciousness. Between reality, whatever it may in actuality be, and our actual intellectual-emotional needs, interests, and capacities, as these are wedded to our sense-based experience, there is a qualitative gap. Our experience is selective; it is timebound; it is culturally conditioned in a variety of ways. Reality, whatever it may be, does not have these characteristics—or, at least, there is no reason to believe that it has or that our ordinary mental equipment is perfectly adapted to and is fully isomorphic with it.

If, for these and other reasons, truth as being is incommensurable with any other meaning of truth that we have or kind of truth that we seek, then an adequate general theory of truth would have to acknowledge at least two realms of truth: an absolute truth as being (whatever reality may in actuality be), and a domain of other truths that is appropriate to our ordinary experience and is applicable to individual beings. The two types of truth need not, however, form a dualism; rather, because of their incommensurability, they give us different *levels* of truth; that is to say, because of their incommensurability no relation as such can be established between truth as being and truth as authentic being (rightness).[3]

According to this ontological theory of truth, then, truth is a quality of an individual object (artwork, linguistic utterance). It is not something external to the object or something that is added to it in virtue of some other quality or relationship that the object may possess. Truth as rightness, rather, is part and parcel of the very being of the thing. The truth of a thing, we argue, is discerned by us as fundamentally as its "primary" qualities. It is grounded in the reality of the thing. The truth of a thing is inseparable from the thing itself in its achieved and achieving state of being.

Truth, then, is not to be found as such in any relation that may obtain between something and something else (e.g., in a "correspondence" between a proposition and a state of affairs); rather, it is to be found as an inherent quality or state of a thing; what the thing itself may be in its actual being. Truth is thus obtained through the articulation of the thing's own intentionality.

II

To bring some previously stated points together:

By the intentionality *of a thing we mean whatever a thing qua the individual thing that it is aims to be by its own nature.*

An artwork, for example, intends its own mode of being as the realization of a special fusion of aesthetic force, significance, and beauty; its aiming to concentrate meaning and form into a dynamic presence. The intentionality of an artwork is its aiming to be a *unique* concentration of value and meaning.

We have said that the intentionality of a thing gives rise to the conditions under which its own authenticity is discerned. We grasp intentionality, not by any mysterious peering into the inside of a thing, but rather by our noticing its "direction," by our recognizing its possible fulfillment as the thing it presents itself as being. The intentionality of an artwork is discerned in terms of our noticing, with whatever content that is available to us, that the artwork is an artwork and is the artwork that it has sought to become. The intentionality of an utterance is determined in terms of our perceiving what the language as language is doing or is trying to do in its particular way within its own mode of functioning.

"Intentionality" suggests aim, direction, purpose, function; as we use the term, "intentionality" is internally constituted in the special way that the particular individual thing itself is.

The truth of a thing calls for its realizing its own rightness through the articulation of its intentionality.

Every thing has its own conditions of being; its time and place, with all that that involves, as a historical being. We cannot imagine an un-differentiated *individual* thing: by the necessities of thought and the constraints of being, individuality calls for historical placement, for all the contingencies associated with the birth and life of the particular thing. A thing must aim to be within the conditions of its being. Although it may try to escape the conditions entirely (through some sort of radical innovation), they nevertheless are the stuff of affirmation and transformation of the individual thing. They are in many ways the limits, the brute factual obduracy, if you will, of the individual thing; they are in all ways of vital importance for the rightness of the thing.

Rightness or authenticity, nevertheless, as we have seen especially for artworks, requires more than the simple affirmation or presentation of the conditions of the thing. The authentic thing is never utterly transparent, a mere presentation of its contingencies; if it were, one would see through it completely to something else (to an idea or stereotype)—or to nothing at all. The authentic thing realizes itself as the thing it ought to be according to its own conditions, which is to say, it must attain to its own integrity of being.

The "ought" here is perhaps troublesome. It is not meant in the sense of "what is permissible" by some ethical or social standard, but of what is right for the individual thing in terms of its own ontological conditions and power of being. Each thing, we are saying, has an integrity—or *excellence*, if you like—that is autochthonously appropriate to it. Each thing has its own intentionality. The inauthentic, the false, is the not-realized, the wrongly formed, the merely borrowed.

But when something is realized, we have rightness as the articulation of intentionality. To articulate an intentionality means to realize explicitly the thing's own aim to be. The realization is within the matrix of the existential conditions of the thing, and it is, necessarily, a dynamic realization. The articulated is not just a finished thing; rather, it is the thing as still open to development, to our discerning new meanings and values in it, to its being "corrected" in the light of new experience. Articulation involves, then, just that spiritual freedom and spontaneity that is so central in the realization of human authenticity. The process of articulation, of realizing intentionality, is eventful and continual.

To sum up at this point: truth, we argue, within the domain of our ordinary sense-mental experience, is rightness. Something is true when it achieves rightness through the articulation of its own intentionality. Truth may be an inherent quality of anything that has the capacity to realize authentic being. And anything that has this capacity has an aim and meaning as just the kind of thing it is as it is a particular thing. It has its immanent objectivity; its drive to be what it ought to be according to its own aim and condition. Rightness requires the realization of the intentionality of the thing within the contingencies, the existential conditions of the thing. Rightness pertains to an individual being in the framework of its own historicity. Rightness means integrity of being: the articulation of an intentionality, the explicit realization, the presentation of the thing as realizing its own aim and power to be what it is. The nature of truth is thus seen as a qualitative achievement. It is not just given; it is attained.

III

We turn now to the *test* for truth. Bertrand Russell felt that the question of the meaning of truth was rather easy to settle but that the question of the test for truth was of "the very greatest difficulty, to which no completely satisfactory answer is possible.''[4] We have stated that: X is determined by Y to be true when Y recognizes that there is no correct alternative to X within the matrix of its presentation—where Y is a person qualified to make the determination that X is true. There are two aspects to this formulation: that of the perception of ''no correct alternative'' (the problem of contradiction), and that of the qualifications of the tester.

To begin with the latter, there is, we would argue, no purely objective, which is to say, there is no simple *mechanical,* test for truth, for all tests (even of 'The cat is on the mat' sort of thing) involve a subject who is open to error and deception, and who must be free from such (and other) factors for truth to be attained. Any test calls for the fulfilling of some conditions on the part of the tester. And the qualifications of the tester in areas such as art and morality can be rather stringent indeed. Because of the requirements of natural sensitivities and dispositions, training and education, not everyone is qualified to determine the rightness of a work of art. We accept this ''aristocratic'' criterion in the sciences (few of us are willing to pronounce for ourselves, i.e., not just repeating some expert's view, on the truth of a theory in physics), but we tend to be wary of it in the value areas of our experience. This wariness is in many ways healthy; for it constrains charlatans posing as experts. But when this wariness becomes pugnacious it is in serious error, as it makes impossible an adequate account of the criteria for testing truth as rightness.

But if the thesis is granted that there are special qualifications for the tester of truth in many areas of our experience, the questions still inevitably arise as to who is to set the qualifications and who is to determine if they have been fulfilled. These (social) questions often reduce to: Who is the ideal tester? and: How he is to be known? The more meaningful (philosophical) question, however, might be: How do we define the competent tester? And the rather simple answer to this is: the competent tester is one who is unbiased to the degree necessary to allow his rational and sensible sensitivities to function in a manner sufficient for, and appropriate to, the object whose truth is in question.

Let us say that Jones has a peculiar mental disposition (based on some weird childhood experience) that compels him to believe that the maximal speed in the universe is that of the speed of light. No conceivable evidence to the contrary would ever or could ever convince him otherwise. As a thinker he would engage in ad hoc hypothesis-making until his last breath rather than admit to the (even possible) error of his belief. Now, it is clear that the truth or falsity of Jones' belief is not in any way related to his peculiar mental condition. We wouldn't look there to find the truth or falsity of the belief, but to science and the world. His compulsion to believe is logically independent of the truth or falsity of the belief itself. To argue otherwise would be to commit the ''genetic fallacy'' in its purest form. But, and here is the point of the illustration, Jones' compulsion to believe is *not* independent of *his* capacity to determine the truth or falsity of his belief and of other related beliefs. His compulsion simply rules out his capacity to discriminate truth from falsity in this area. He would thus be an incompetent tester.

The competent tester would be one who is unbiased to the degree necessary to do his work; which means to the degree necessary to allow his sensitivities to function in a manner appropriate to the object whose truth is being tested. Just to be unbiased is clearly not enough to qualify as a tester of truth; it is a necessary but not sufficient condition. Competency also requires that one have adequate knowledge and experience. And we need not specify all the ingredients (and to what amount) that may go to make for this adequacy; we do not need to provide a recipe for this in order for the philosophical point to be established that any account of the test for truth must include the matter of the unbiased competency of the tester.

Turning now to the problem of contradiction: What does it mean to recognize that there is no correct alternative to something within the matrix of its presentation? With artworks, we saw that when we discern integrity we accept and affirm the work as being right for itself. We recognize that it is necessary as it is; that it has attained to what it should be according to its own ''ought'' to be. We contradict, on the other hand, we recognize that a work is inauthentic or false, when we perceive that the object is not doing what it intends to do, that it is not what it pretends to be; when, in short, we recognize that it needs to be replaced in its own being with another possibility that would be right for it.[5]

Contradiction here means rejecting something within the conditions and intentionality of the thing itself. Contradiction here does not mean the actual replacement of an object or state of being by another qualitatively different object or state of being, as was the case with "truth as being" (and is the case generally with the establishment of ontological levels of being); it means, by virtue of the perception of a lack of rightness of the thing, the recognition that the thing needs to be replaced by another actuality for it—within its own conditions and intentionality.

The test for (and guarantee of) truth, we maintain, is thus noncontradictoriness: with the locus of contradiction being the object itself; that is to say, we determine rightness, not by some external standard, but in terms of the object's own intentionality. The authentic thing is what is right for itself. We test its truth just by perceiving its rightness and by judging if there is a correct alternative to it within the matrix of its own realized being.

Conclusion
The Value of Truth

TRUTH is an excellence (an *aretē* if you will) of any thing. Truth, we maintain, is as "objective" as the sensible qualities of a thing; and it is also a value—a valuable accomplishment of the thing.

How valuable is truth? To answer this one has only to imagine what the world would be like in its absence. If nothing could ever be what it ought to be according to its own intentionality—whether because of some congenital limitation or some externally imposed constraint—so that a nonempty concept of truth could not even be formulated, we would have a world that was valueless. For truth is not just a value among values; rather, it has a privileged status in that its existence is necessary for other values to be realized. Aesthetic and moral sensitivity surely depend upon and presuppose it, for truth is precisely what much of that sensitivity is directed toward. If artworks could not achieve integrity; if religious language could not reveal, guide, or be rightly formative of consciousness; if propositions could not present facts, then justice, loyalty, honesty—the whole range of "virtues"—could not exist. They would not have, as it were, a locus.

And hence the philosopher's abiding interest in truth—both formally, as that which is conceived (the nature and test of truth), and substantively, as that which is sought (as artful understanding).

But let us not, while acknowledging its privileged status, *over*value truth (as rightness). For, in the final analysis, philosophical lucidity does involve the recognition of the untruth of all things; a recognition that is by no means commonplace, as it is more than an intellectual assent to some kind of arid skepticism or relativism—it is a blinding insight into the fulness of being, which insight is, at the same time, an awareness of the truth of being.

Truth of being is inaccessible to philosophy, insofar as thought must be a *thinking about;* which is to say, an *objectifying* process. Truth of being, to borrow an old simile, is for us like our eyes which can't see themselves but which nevertheless enable us to see; it is the ground from which all right thinking arises—and to which all thinking ought to return.

Truth is silence. The truth of being is nameless, but more than that it simply reduces all sound to nothingness. And so, one can only seek to realize that *freedom* of being which is, in our human terms, the very truth of being.

Notes

INTRODUCTION

1. *The Logic of Hegel,* trans. William Wallace, from the *Encyclopaedia of the Philosophical Sciences* (Oxford: The Clarendon Press, 1892), p. 305.

2. G. W. F. Hegel, *The Phenomenology of Mind,* trans. J. B. Baillie (New York: Harper & Row, Harper Torchbooks, 1967), p. 71.

3. Wallace, *Logic,* p. 354.

4. Hegel, *Phenomenology,* p. 81.

5. Charles Taylor, *Hegel* (Cambridge: Cambridge University Press, 1975), p. 328.

6. Stanley Rosen, *G. W. F. Hegel: An Introduction to the Science of Wisdom* (New Haven and London: Yale University Press, 1974), p. 239.

7. J. L. Mehta, *Martin Heidegger: The Way and the Vision* (Honolulu: The University Press of Hawaii, 1976), p. 189.

8. Martin Heidegger, "On the Essence of Truth," trans. R. F. C. Hull and Alan Crick, in *Existence and Being,* ed. Werner Brock (Chicago: Henry Regnery Co., 1949), p. 322. See also Heidegger's *Platons Lehre von der Wahrheit. Mit einer Brief uber den "Humanismus"* (Bern: A. Franck, 1947).

9. Heidegger, "On the Essence of Truth," p. 323.

10. Ibid., p. 329.

11. Ibid., pp. 328–329.

12. Ibid., p. 329.

13. Ibid., p. 330.

14. Ibid., p. 331.

15. Ibid., p. 333.

16. Mehta, *Heidegger,* p. 190.

17. Cf. Aristotle, *Metaphysics* 1011.26.

18. Albert Hofstadter, *Truth and Art* (New York and London: Columbia University Press, 1965), p. 92.

19. Ibid., p. 97.

20. Ibid., p. 108.

21. Ibid., p. 103.

22. Ibid., p. 105.

23. Ibid., p. 110.

24. Ibid., p. 113.

25. Ibid., p. 121.

26. Ibid., pp. 128–129.

27. Ibid., pp. 136–137.

28. Ibid., p. 137.
29. Ibid., p. 138.
30. Ibid., p. 140.
31. Wallace, "Logic," p. 253.
32. Hofstadter, *Truth and Art,* p. 212.

CHAPTER I

1. This, of course, is the conventional (and rather oversimplified) understanding of Plato's position, which ought to be tempered somewhat by taking into account the "historical situation" at Plato's time concerning the relationship between the philosopher and the poet. For a helpful account of this see Whitney J. Oates, *Plato's View of Art* (New York: Charles Scribner's Sons, 1972), chap. 1.

2. *Poetics* 1460[b].

3. R. K. Elliot, for example, has argued that aesthetic experience involves setting up relations between the artwork's meaning and the participant's past experience, and that "establishing the meaning is itself verification." For "If the poet is successful the meaning of the poetic sentences extends to cover the phenomenon. . . . As soon as the phenomenon has been brought to intuition and, as it were, named by the poetic sentences these sentences are grasped as having described it truly" ("Poetry and Truth," *Analysis* 27, no. 3 [January 1967]).

Alexander Sesonske also argues that in some arts at least truth may be relevant and even essential to aesthetic experience. Although it is not "the function of art to discover and convey new truths," the aesthetic import of many works "is heightened by our awareness of the truth of what is expressed." ("Truth in Art," *The Journal of Philosophy* 53, no. 11 [May 1956]).

Bertram E. Jessup ("Truth as Material in Art," *The Journal of Aesthetics and Art Criticism* [hereafter *JAAC*] 4, no. 2 [Winter 1945]); F. E. Sparshott ("Truth in Fiction," *JAAC* 26, no. 1, [Fall 1967]); and James K. Feibleman ("The Truth Value of Art," *JAAC* 24, no. 4 [Summer 1966]) also support, in varying ways, the position that truth in art is aesthetically relevant, with Sparshott arguing the larger case that imagination, via memory, always works with the actual world so that "truth" is always relevant in art, and Feibleman that there are many truth-values in art (the truth-value of coherence, when the work has unity, as well as correspondence, when it deals with "the axiological aspects of facts").

Somewhat greater weight, though, seems to be cast on the other side of the argument. Douglas N. Morgan ("Must Art Tell the Truth," *JAAC* 26, no. 1 [Fall 1967]), among many others, has forcefully argued that "truth" indeed pertains only to propositions, but that art does not need justification on truth grounds at all. Its value as beauty is sufficient. Albert William Levi ("Literary Truth," *JAAC* 24, no. 3 [Spring 1966]) (following somewhat more closely the position I. A. Richards put forward in *Science and Poetry* [1926] and *Principles of Literary Criticism* [1925] takes the same line and insists that "truth" rightly belongs to logic and science and that it is a category mistake to apply it to art (literature). "Meaning," "significance" are different from "truth" and do apply to the autonomous domain of the creative imagination.

Kingsley Price ("Is There Artistic Truth?" *The Journal of Philosophy* 66, no. 2 [May 1949]) (". . . works of art do not mean other things to which they might be true"); Sidney Zink ("Poetry and Truth," *The Philosophical Review* 54, no. 2 [1945]) ("Truth is not something to be contemplated, nor even something to be 'enforced', in the sense of persuaded. Truth is rather to be discovered or verified. And because it is not the business of poetry to discover or verify, poems *as* poems, are neither true nor false"); and Louis Arnaud Reid ("Art, Truth and Reality," *The British Journal of Aesthetics* 4, no. 4 [October 1964]) ("Whereas the criterion of truth as likeness sets up a prior model of natural fact to which the picture is supposed to correspond, just the reverse happens when the art is good. The art itself becomes and sets the standard by which the world is seen in a new way")—develop this position further.

4. Albert Hofstadter, *Truth and Art* (New York: Columbia University Press, 1965), pp. 179–180.

5. Gerardus van der Leeuw, *Sacred and Profane Beauty: The Holy in Art*, trans. David E. Green (New York: Holt, Rinehart & Winston, 1963), p. 11. Cf. also Wladyslaw Tatarkiewicz, *History of Aesthetics*, ed. J. Harrell (The Hague: Mouton and Warsaw: Polish Scientific Publishers, 1970), 1:16 ff.

6. By a "traditional" culture or stage of culture I mean that mode of social-intellectual-spiritual life wherein, through a heightened self-consciousness and ability to communicate values, a shared literature (oral or written) of myth, poem, and dogma is established.

7. Part of the basis for the separation is undoubtedly to be found in the belief of organized religion that it can, with the advance of its own symbolic means of expression in the form of concepts, dispense with art and indeed even oppose it as something which may stand in the way of religious consciousness. Herbert Read describes the process nicely in this way: "Ritual implies art—it needs art for the creation of its ritualistic objects. Religious emotion, too, must be generated by ritualistic objects. So far art and religion are interdependent. At the stage of the formulation of belief, art may or may not be necessary; it will prove at any rate useful for the formulation of symbols, the shorthand of beliefs, and for intructional purposes—as a pictorial language for the illiterate. But at the rationalizing stage of religion, when religion becomes more than anything else an affair of philosophical concepts and of individual meditation, then there is bound to grow up a feeling that religion can dispense with such sensuous representations as works of art—indeed, such objects will come to be regarded as definitely antagonistic to the life of the spirit" ("Art and Religion," *Listener*, 5 August 1936).

8. Leonard B. Meyer, *Emotion and Meaning in Music* (Chicago: The University of Chicago Press, 1956), p. 34.

9. Octavio Paz, *The Bow and the Lyre*, trans. Ruth L. C. Simms (Austin and London: University of Texas Press, 1973), p. 142.

10. Susanne K. Langer, *Feeling and Form* (New York: Charles Scribner's Sons, 1953), p. 311.

11. See Siegfried Krocauer, *Theory of Film: The Redemption of Physical Reality* (Oxford: Oxford University Press, 1960).

12. John J. Martin, *An Introduction to the Dance* (New York: W. W. Norton & Co., 1939), p. 62.

13. Ibid., p. 63.

14. Morris Weitz, "The Role of Theory in Aesthetics," *Journal of Aesthetics and Art Criticism* 15, no. 1 (September 1956): 27–35.

The most radical—and, with its curt dismissal of any intrinsic aesthetic values in art, perhaps the most aesthetically barren—formulation of this attitude is presented in the view (Danto, Dickie, etc.) that a work of art is not defined by any qualities (family-resemblancelike or otherwise) it may possess but simply according to what (certain) persons are willing to call a work of art within a certain social or institutional context. If a museum exhibits a pile of dirt thrown randomly on the floor with someone's (presumably the thrower's) signature attached to it (perhaps also with a price tag), then it simply is a work of art. The concept "work of art" does not thus apply to objects which may share certain features but to anything that is legitimized (baptized) in the so-called art world as a bearer of the concept. See Arthur Danto, "The Artworld," *Journal of Philosophy,* 1964, pp. 571–584; George Dickie, *Aesthetics: An Introduction* (Bobbs-Merrill Co., Pegasus, 1971), chap. 11.

15. *American Philosophical Quarterly* 2, no. 3 (July 1965): 219–228.

16. W. D. Ross, *Aristotle* (New York: Meridian Books, 1959), p. 269.

Harvey D. Goldstein, in an interesting article, "Mimesis and Catharsis Reexamined" (*The Journal of Aesthetics and Art Criticism* 24, no. 4 [Summer 1966], 567–777), points out, however, that Aristotle did also use mimesis to convey the idea of copying but that mimesis had for Aristotle primarily to do with an imitation of the *method* or *process* of nature and not with a representation of sense-objects.

17. Plotinus, *Enneads* 5.8.1, trans. Stephen MacKenna.

18. Katharine Everett Gilbert and Helmut Kuhn, *A History of Esthetics* (Bloomington, Ind.: Indiana University Press, 1953), p. 220.

19. Leo Steinberg, "The Eye Is a Part of the Mind," in *Reflections on Art,* ed. Susanne K. Langer (New York: Oxford University Press, 1961), p. 245.

But Steinberg goes on to set up a straw man as an opponent to this view by arguing that the only alternative to "art is imitation," which he then explains is largely a symbolic process ("Representation in art is the fashioning of graphic symbols to act as analogues for certain areas of visual experience") is some peculiar notion that art operates in a complete void and is thus creative *ex nihilo.*

20. Langer, *Feeling and Form,* p. 46.

In his *Art and Scholasticism,* Jacques Maritain also notes: "The truth is, it is difficult to determine in what precisely this imitation-copy consists, the concept of which seems so clear to minds which have their being among the simplified schemata of the popular imagination.

"Is it the imitation or the copy of what the thing in itself *is* and its intelligible *type?* But that is an object of conception, not of sensation . . . which art, consequently, cannot directly reproduce. Is it the imitation or the copy of the *sensations* produced in us by the thing? But the sensations attain the consciousness of each one of us only as refracted by an inner atmosphere of memories and emotions, and are, moreover, eternally changing in a flux in which all things become distorted and are continuously intermingled; so that from the point of view of *pure sensation* it must be admitted with the Futurists that a 'galloping horse has not four hoofs but twenty. . . .'

"The reproduction or exact copy of nature thus appears as the object of an impossible pursuit—a concept which vanishes when an attempt is made to define it."

21. Tatarkiewicz, *History*, p. 17.

22. Clive Bell, *Art* (London: Chatto & Windus, 1928), p. 16.

23. "Only through the pure contemplation . . . which ends entirely in the object, can Ideas be comprehended, and the nature of *genius* consists in pre-eminent capacity for such contemplation. Now, as this requires that a man should entirely forget himself and the relations in which he stands, *genius* is simply the completest *objectivity*, i.e., the objective tendency of the mind, as opposed to the subjective, which is directed to one's own self. . . ." 3:36.

24. This account of imagination is, of course, exactly contra to Freud's treatment of creativity in art, insofar as Freud assumes that this creativity is reducible to a kind of compensatory satisfaction-seeking, a fulfillment of desires that are denied the artist in the real world. Art becomes then a manifestation of wish-fulfilling desires and is responded to precisely in those terms. Cf. his "The Relation of the Poet to Day-Dreaming." It is interesting to note that everything that Freud says about art is true—for bad art or for merely popular fantasy stuff like so-called soap operas.

25. Cf. Vincent Tomas, "Creativity in Art," *The Philosophical Review* 67, no. 1 (January 1958), and Monroe C. Beardsley, "On the Creation of Art," *The Journal of Aesthetics and Art Criticism* 23, no. 3 (1965).

26. And hence the sense in the assertion often made that artistic creativity is an articulation or self-formation of the artist as much as it is the making of an artwork. Creativity in art forms the artist; it is a kind of self-*discovery* and self-*making*, not a mere self-*expression*. The creativity of an artist is thus often as much a suprise to him as it may be a wonder to others.

27. R. G. Collingwood, *The Principles of Art* (Oxford: The Clarendon Press, 1938), p. 120.

The expression theory of art has undergone an interesting and rather curious historical development. Spawned by romanticism's emphasis on the artist as a self-consciously *creative* being, with art often looked upon as a means for his self-expression, the theory, in its initial formulations (by Eugène Vérnon, Croce, Collingwood, Ducasse) was concerned primarily with the creative process, willing as it was at times (e.g., Croce) to relegate the actual physical work of art to a secondary position. The making of an artwork, in the initial formulation, was a kind of therapy. It enabled the artist, and the experiencer of his art, to attain a knowledge of, and by implication a freedom from, an otherwise turbulent, inchoate emotional force.

Thinkers like Susanne K. Langer, however, recognized that as a psychology of the creative process the traditional expression theory is severely limited to at best a particular type of creativity and insisted, in a more sophisticated way, that the artwork may be a symbol of human feeling. The artwork then becomes an expressive form—an articulation of feeling for contemplative understanding.

It wasn't long before analytically oriented philosophers (Monroe Beardsley, O. K. Bouswma, John Hospers) discovered a lack of clarity in the whole notion of expression, that the terms 'express,' 'expressive,' and 'expression' were used in a wide variety of ways. The critics shifted the whole direction of the theory away from the artist and toward the expressive values of the artwork itself by asking how we can intelligibly ascribe anthropomorphic qualities to a work of art ("sad music" as the saw or paradigm). And they concluded that the expression theory was utterly dispensable. All expression-language used to talk about artworks can be translated without loss of meaning into non-expression-language (about formal qualities and subject matter).

In very recent times, however, other analytically oriented writers (Alan Tormay, *The Concept of Expression* [Princeton: Princeton University Press, 1971]; Guy Sircello, *Mind and Art: An Essay on the Varieties of Expression* [Princeton: Princeton University Press, 1972]) have tried to rescue the theory by appealing to various ways in which anthropomorphic predicates can be applied to works of art in a manner unlike their application to natural objects, and thus to show how 'expression,' 'expressive of,' and 'expressing' are necessary for aesthetic analysis. The emphasis, however, still remains on how it can be said that a work of art is expressive of certain human emotions. The theory is perhaps ready now for a more basic reconstruction—at the roots.

28. John Hospers, "The Concept of Artistic Expression," reprinted with some changes by the author in *Problems of Aesthetics,* ed. Morris Weitz (New York: Macmillan Co., 1970).

29. Ibid., p. 227.

30. Susanne K. Langer, "Problems of Art," in *A Modern Book of Esthetics,* ed. Melvin Rader, 4th ed. (New York: Holt, Rinehart & Winston, 1973), p. 296.

31. Vincent Tomas, an excerpt from *Science, Language and Human Rights,* reprinted in *Philosophy Looks at the Arts,* ed. Joseph Margolis (New York: Charles Scribner's Sons, 1962), p. 31.

32. Ibid., p. 43.

33. Nelson Goodman, in his *Languages of Art* (New York: The Bobbs-Merrill Co., 1968), raises the interesting question about the "localization" of a work of art. He argues that "a musical score is in a notation and defines a work; that a sketch or picture is not in a notation but is itself a work; and that a literary script is both in a notation and is itself a work. Thus in the different arts a work is differently localized. In painting, the work is an individual object; and in etching, a class of objects. In music, the work is the class of performances compliant with a character. In literature, the work is the character itself. And in calligraphy, we may add, the work is an individual inscription" (p. 210).

But what Goodman fails to realize is that an artwork, as localized, is always in a particular creative-experiential cultural context—and that this context is part and parcel of the identification of the work qua particular, localized work. There is, in short, an "autographic" element in every work of art (in music, for instance, we are not interested in exact and thereby repetitious readings of a score, as though the ideal would be to have identical performances). Also, the way in which it is appropriate to respond to a particular work is essential to its identification. If we had a case of two apparently identical works from different cultures, it would nevertheless make perfectly good sense to say that they were not the *same* work. See Anthony Savile, "Nelson Goodman's 'Languages of Art': A Study," *The British Journal of Aesthetics* 11, no. 1 (Winter 1971), for an interesting analysis of this point.

34. In a famous essay " 'Psychical Distance' as a Factor in Art and an Aesthetic Principle," (*British Journal of Psychology* 5 [1912]), Edward Bullough argued that aesthetic

experience demands the insertion of a certain distance "between our own self and its af-fections" or "between our self and such objects as are the sources or vehicles of such af-fections." This distance is obtained, Bullough says, "by separating the object and its appeal from one's own self, by putting it out of gear with practical needs and ends." He goes on to say that "Distance does not imply an impersonal, purely intellectually inter-ested relation of such a kind. On the contrary, it describes a *personal* relation, often highly emotionally colored, but of a *peculiar character.* Its peculiarity lies in that the personal character of the relation has been, so to speak, filtered. It has been cleared of the practical, concrete nature of its appeal, without, however, thereby losing its original constitution." He concludes by postulating an "antinomy of Distance," namely, that "What is therefore, both in appreciation and production, most desirable is *the utmost decrease of Distance without its disappearance.*" This allows the participant to be deep-ly involved with the artwork yet able to relate with it precisely as it is a work of art. Now although there are many ambiguities and difficulties in this notion of a "psychical dis-tance," it—or something like it—has become widely accepted as describing the *attitude* appropriate to our experience of artworks.

35. Bell, *Art,* p. 4.

36. Dorothy Walsh, "The Cognitive Content of Art," *The Philosophical Review* 52, no. 4 (September 1943).

37. Hofstadter, *Truth and Art,* pp. 195–196.

38. Ibid., p. 140.

39. Roderick Chisholm developed a "linguistic version" of Brentano's thesis in his effort to set forth criteria for the intentional use of language; that is, language which refers to certain psychological states. "Intentionality" here has fundamentally to do with our talking about various kinds of mental phenomena. It applies both to mental states and events and to the sentences that are required to describe these states and events. Intentional sentences are those that meet certain criteria that are not exhibited by sentences employed to describe "physical" phenomena. Cf. "Sentences About Be-lieving," in *Minnesota Studies in the Philosophy of Science,* ed. H. Feigl, M. Scriven, and G. Maxwell (Minneapolis: University of Minnesota Press, 1958), vol. 2.

40. Susanna Winkworth, trans., *Theologia Germanica* (New York: Pantheon Books, 1949), p. 124.

41. We must, of course, allow for the situation where one might be so repulsed by a world view or particular subject matter (say a graphic depiction of a horrible infanticide) that one simply rejects the work from the start. In this case, though, it is not a matter of disagreeing with the work aesthetically because of its view; it is a matter of not getting to the work as an aesthetic object in the first place.

42. *Time,* 24 January 1955, p. 72.

43. Alan White, *Truth* (New York: Doubleday & Co., Anchor Books, 1970), p. 115.

44. In his careful analysis of the problem of forgeries, Nelson Goodman shows very nicely how knowledge of the fact of a forgery, where there is no apparent perceptual dif-ference between the original and the forgery, nevertheless can make for an aesthetic dif-ference, because the knowledge "(1) stands as evidence that there may be a difference between them that I can learn to perceive, (2) assigns the present looking a role as train-ing toward such a perceptual discrimination, and (3) makes consequent demands that

modify and differentiate my present experience in looking at the two pictures" *(Languages of Art* [New York: The Bobbs-Merrill Co., 1968] p. 105*).* Goodman, however, draws the rather curious conclusion that the "aesthetic difference" does not mean that an original is necessarily better than the forgery ("a copy of a Lastman by Rembrandt may well be better than the original"); and this confusion, I believe, arises once again from Goodman's failure to realize that an artwork is definable only when taking into account the creative process which brought it into being and the experience appropriate to it. The artwork, we have argued, is a process and a completion; it is grounded, it is rooted in its "existential conditions." A forgery can never fulfill properly the intentionality of art. A master artist does not "copy" another work (if he did so as some sort of exercise, he would not regard it as a work); he may seek to be influenced by another work, but the 'own work' which may then be superior to the "original" is precisely a new work and not a copy of something else. It would have its own authenticity.

45. A similar situation exists in those cases where one is fooled by an artwork in taking it for the "real" thing. The critic Harold Rosenberg states the situation nicely in this way: "The interval during which a painting is mistaken for the real thing, or a real thing for a painting, is the triumphant moment of trompe l'oeil art. The artist appears to be as potent as nature, if not superior to it. Almost immediately, though, the spectator's uncertainty is eliminated by his recognition that the counterfeit is counterfeit. Once the illusion is dissolved, what is left is an object that is interesting, not as a work of art, but as a successful simulation of something that is not art. The major response to it is curiosity. ("The Art World: Reality Again," *The New Yorker,* 5 February 1972, p. 88.)

46. White, *Truth,* p. 118.

CHAPTER II

1. Paul Ziff insists that "the English utterance 'God exists' occurs in religious discourses in English (not in 'religious language'—there is no such thing)." (Cf. "About 'God'," in *Religious Experience and Truth,* ed. Sidney Hook [New York: New York University Press, 1961], p. 195.) Although Ziff is technically correct (in the sense that linguists do not divide languages into "religious" or other modes), I wish nevertheless to retain the expression "religious language," much like scientists and philosophers of science do "scientific language," in order to point out more effectively the *distinctive* qualities of this domain of language and language use. These qualities are so readily lost, it seems, in much analytic philosophy that dispenses with the general category.

The three types within the general category, we must also note, are not intended to exhaust the category. Other types of religious language might indeed be distinguished. The three types we have selected, however, are of central importance in any classification and seem to us to best allow us to get at the issue of truth in religious language. Further, it is understood throughout the analysis that in actuality language does not come to us ready for labeling into neat classifications. Utterances will move across our categories with relative ease, sometimes exhibiting greater affinity with one type, at other times with another type, and so on. But the special features distinguished still stand as marking off types of language use in religion and enable us, it is hoped, to grasp the truth-dimension of religious language.

2. This is recognized in many religious traditions, but perhaps nowhere more fully

than in the Brahmanic culture of India. Together with the notion that the word is the ground of all being (*śabda brahman*—the word as source of the world) the Upaniṣads recognize the utterly transcendent quality of ontological silence. Cf. *Taittīrīya Upaniṣad* 2.4.1: *"yato vaco nivartante, aprāpya manasā saha."* ("*[Brahman is that] from whence words return along with the mind not attaining it.*") Buddhism, too, offers this realization in many forms. E.g., *nivṛttam abhidhatavyaṃ nivṛtte cittagocara.* "When the domain of thought has been dissipated, 'that which can be stated' is dissipated." Nāgārjuna, *Mūlamadhyamakakārikās* 18.7, trans. Frederick J. Streng.

3. And hence the distinction that needs to be made between so-called primitive religiosity and higher forms of spirituality. With the primitive (as an elementary form of religion and not as an anthropological type) we have word magic: the investing of certain sounds with extraordinary power and the fearful and aweful response to, and attempt to gain control of, them (and through them to what they might stand for). In this case, the spiritual self is absent and the empirical self is entirely there.

Nevertheless there is something positive in the primitive mode which as we lose it today leads only to our own impoverishment, and that is its profound recognition of the inherent potentialities of language to express spiritual power. We have so developed abstract relations and ideas that have no intrinsic relation to what they stand for, being entirely conventional in character, that we can only with the utmost difficulty even appreciate this other attitude. But assuredly one of the wonders of language is just its potentiality to be revelatory; to express directly the rhythm of spiritual being through insight and love.

4. When I speak of religious "language *of* " as revelation, I am not conceiving of revelation just on a Western model of something that is given or delivered by a God. I want precisely to avoid having an analysis of religious language turn on either a commitment to, or a rejection of, theism per se (as most analyses clearly do). As I understand it, revelation is just the presentation of spiritual being by means of the intrinsic rhythmic quality and spiritual grounding of a language. Religious "language *of* " can thus be true without its being the whole of truth. When a claim for the whole of truth is made in religion, we have, as Tillich might say, an idolatrous distortion of religious "language *of* "—if not an outright metaphysical absurdity. Religious "language *of* " is distorted—is false—when, while trying, it fails to be presentative of spiritual being and when it makes claims for finality or ultimacy for itself. Religious "language *of,* " like all language, always retains the characteristic of "pointing to" as well as "partaking of" spiritual being.

5. Religious "language *for*" is often exhibited in distorted ways precisely because of the inability of the speaker to meet these conditions of nonegoistic openness to, and sympathetic concern with, the other. The religious *performer,* whether he be a priest, professor, or swami, like most performers, speaks *to* or *at* his audience more for the sake of their praiseful response than for their to-be-realized state of being. In these cases we have pseudo-"language-*for*": we have language that tells us about the speaker, not language that is for the spoken to.

6. Plotinus, *Enneads* 4.8.4, trans. Stephen MacKenna.

7. This second factor of pragmatic efficacy, in many instances, takes precedence over the first and sometimes becomes the sole criterion for truth in religious "language *for.* " In Buddhism, for example, there are many teachings where correspondence truth-value

is set aside and the entire weight is placed on pragmatic-spiritual efficacy. See the "Parable of the Burning House" and others in *Saddharma Pandarīka*. Also cf. "The Progressive Teaching Technique of the Gītā" in my *The Bhagavad Gītā* (New York: Holt, Rinehart & Winston, 1968), pp. 20–22.

8. *Of Learned Ignorance,* trans. Fr. Germain Heron (London: Routledge & Kegan Paul, 1954), p. 11.

9. The difficulties in formulating an adequate criterion of verifiability have, of course, proven to be formidable. For a good historical account of this see Carl Hemple, "Problems and Changes in the Empiricist Criterion of Meaning," in *Révue internationale de philosophie* 4 (1950): 41–62.

10. See the criticisms of Kai Nielson in his article "Eschatological Verification," *Canadian Journal of Philosophy* 9 (1963).

11. The influence of positivism in theology and philosophy of religion has been enormous and rather remarkable. For a good bibliography of the rather vast literature dealing with the positivist-influenced problems of the cognitive meaningfulness and logical status of religious language [about] see James I. Campbell, *The Language of Religion* (New York: Bruce Publishing Co.; London: Collier-Macmillan, 1971), pp. 164 ff. It was as if (Protestant) theologians all along were suspicious that they weren't quite talking sense and just needed the prod of the positivist's sword (and analyst's stick) to set them to work finding ways in which their "language *about*" could indeed be cognitively meaningful or, failing this, to find substitutes for being so meaningful.

12. Paul Tillich, *Dynamics of Faith* (New York: Harper & Row, Harper Torchbooks, 1958), p. 41. Tillich's treatment of symbols is covered in a variety of places (and in somewhat different ways) in his many writings. The formulation that we briefly allude to here is a reasonably late one and is sufficiently general for our purpose.

13. Ibid., p. 44.

14. Ibid., p. 96.

15. Ibid., p. 97. In his *Systematic Theology* (Chicago: University of Chicago Press, 1951), 1:240, Tillich also says that "the truth of a religious symbol has nothing to do with the truth of the empirical assertions involved in it, be they physical, psychological, or historical. A religious symbol possesses some truth if it adequately expresses the correlation of revelation in which some person stands."

16. Ibid., pp. 97–98; and, of course, in much of his other work.

17. One of the interesting and very curious theological movements which has been deeply concerned with the nature of religious language and the role of symbols in religious discourse is that of the recent "Death of God" theology. Many of the thinkers connected with this movement (William Hamilton, Thomas J. J. Altizer, Gabriel Vahanian) seem to have taken Tillich very seriously indeed when he spoke of "God as the symbol of God," but they refused to accept Tillich's notion that the symbols must be judged on "objective" as well as (pragmatic) "subjective" grounds. They tore the symbol free from any ontological grounding, and could thus speak about a "death" of the symbol and that to which it points. For an interesting account of the "death of God" as itself a religious symbol see Wilfred Cantwell Smith, *Questions of Religious Truth* (New York: Charles Scribner's Sons, 1967), pp. 13 ff.

18. Eric L. Mascall, *Existence and Analogy* (London: Longmans, Green and Co., 1949), p. 107.

19. Ibid., p. 104.

20. Ibid., p. 110.

21. John E. Smith, *The Analogy of Experience: An Approach to Understanding Religious Truth* (New York: Harper & Row, 1973), p. 53.

22. Ibid., p. 44.

23. Ibid., p. 51.

24. Ibid., p. 53.

25. Ibid., pp. 53–54.

26. Ibid., p. 52.

27. Ibid., p. 105. Some recent philosophic discussion of analogy (which has incorporated contemporary advances in linguistic theory) has taken an interesting direction away from the question of knowledge about God to be obtained through analogy to that of the existence of a "continuity of meaning" between religious discourse and "discourse environments whose cognitive significance is not sensibly to be questioned." See James F. Ross, "Analogy and the Resolution of Some Cognitivity Problems," *The Journal of Philosophy* 67, no. 20 (22 October 1970): 725–746.

28. This does not mean, though, that religious "language *about*" is reducible in some way to religious "language *for.*" The latter is an interpersonal teaching, a mapping of the way for another; the former is more exactly "subjective," functioning for the self's own formation.

29. It is a peculiar characteristic of the relationship between self and language that consciousness becomes, as it were, the form-and-style of the language that is employed (e.g., writing memos or poetry, lecturing, writing personal letters). It is not that the self uses a language and stands off untouched by it; rather, the language as it is employed conditions the user and contributes to the determination of his being during (and often for a considerable time after) its use.

30. Martin Buber, *Eclipse of God* (New York: Harper & Row, Harper Torchbooks, 1957), p. 35.

31. Ibid.

32. Ibid., p. 37.

33. Søren Kierkegaard, *Concluding Unscientific Postscript,* trans. David F. Swenson and Walter Lowrie (Princeton: Princeton University Press, 1941), p. 178.

34. Ibid., p. 182.

35. Rudolph Bultmann, "What Sense Is There to Speak of God?" *The Christian Scholar* 43 (1962): 214.

CHAPTER III

1. This insight follows historically upon the discovery of the difficulties in traditional reference theories of meaning (which argue for the dependency of meaning upon reference) and upon the recognition of the inadequacies in positivist-empiricist efforts to set forth a criterion of meaningfulness based on "verifiability." In his famous work "On Sense and Nominatum," (trans. Herbert Feigl, in *Readings in Philosophical Analysis,* eds. Herbert Feigl and Wilfrid Sellars [New York: Appleton-Century-Crofts, 1949]) Frege argues that "Now it is plausible to connect with a sign (name, word coordination, expression) not only the designated object, which may be called the nominatum ["refer-

ence," or *Bedeutung*] of the sign, but also the sense (connotation, meaning) *[Sinn]* of the sign in which is contained the manner and context of presentation. . . . We let a sign *express* its sense and designate its nominatum." Two expressions, Frege shows, such as "the morning star" and "the evening star," can have the same referent, namely, the planet Venus, but have different senses.

Bertrand Russell in his now classic example of " 'Sir Walter Scott' and 'the author of Waverly' " also showed how two different expressions or terms can have the same referent but very different meanings. And, it is further frequently pointed out, there are a number of key linguistic terms and expressions; e.g., the conjunction 'and', which do not refer to anything and yet are clearly meaningful.

The meaning of an expression, therefore, cannot consist in its just referring to a certain object. Meaning is not coextensive with reference. Nor, it is now widely recognized, can "meaning" be stipulated (rather arbitrarily) to apply only to certain kinds of expressions. The various positivist-empiricist criteria of meaningfulness do just that and yield gross oversimplifications; e.g., the dividing of all expressions into the "cognitive-meaningful" and the "emotive," the "cognitive-meaningful" being restricted to those statements which in principle are verifiable by reference to sense-experience, with everything else being put into the "emotive." Countless sentences—e.g., interrogative sentences—are also clearly meaningful in communities of language-users without being empirically verifiable, and so on.

It is also rather clearly the case that there is no typical unit of meaning as such. Different types of expression may have meaning—and for convenience' sake we may call these different sorts of expressions "utterances." We need not be concerned, then, with the meaning of words as such. Simple word meanings (dictionary synonymity) *by themselves* have no illocutionary force, as we shall see, and, for that matter, perform no locutionary act. We are concerned with meaning only in the context of utterances.

2. See H. P. Grice, "Meaning," in *Philosophical Review* 66 (July 1957): 377–388.

3. Stephen R. Schiffer, *Meaning* (Oxford: Clarendon Press, 1972), p. 7.

4. Ibid.

5. In his well-known *How to Do Things with Words*, ed. J. O. Urmson (New York: Oxford University Press, 1973), John Austin distinguished three kinds of linguistic activities: the *locutionary* act, the *illocutionary* act, and the *perlocutionary* act. The *locutionary* has to do with 'meaning' in the traditional sense; it is the "uttering a certain sentence with a certain sense and reference" (p. 100). The *illocutionary,* on the other hand, has to do with what a particular utterance itself is doing—it may be asserting, ordering, informing, warning, and so on. The illocutionary is bound up with the locutionary, but it is what the speaker wants to do with his utterance. It is his "performance of an act *in* saying something as opposed to performance of an act *of* saying something . . ." (p. 79). By the *perlocutionary* Austin means the actual effects that are produced by an utterance upon those who receive it. "Saying something," Austin writes, "will often, or even normally, produce certain consequential effects upon the feelings, thoughts, or actions of the audience, or of the speaker, or of other persons . . ." (p. 101).

6. See William K. Wimsatt and Monroe C. Beardsley, "The Intentional Fallacy," in *The Verbal Icon* (Lexington: University of Kentucky Press), chap. 1.

7. John R. Searle, *Speech Acts: An Essay in the Philosophy of Language* (Cambridge: At the University Press, 1969), p. 37.

8. Ibid., p. 33.

9. Ibid., p. 34.

10. Ibid., p. 33.

11. Ibid., p. 34.

12. Ibid., p. 44. William P. Alston, in his *Philosophy of Language* (Englewood Cliffs, N.J.: Prentice-Hall, 1964), also accepts and considerably develops this argument.

13. Ibid., p. 47.

14. Ibid., p. 48.

15. Ibid., p. 45.

16. A proposition, however, doesn't have to be true in order to be meaningful; it has only to exhibit its intention to be a proposition, which is to say, it must be recognizable as an assertion about what is thought to be the case.

17. Other conditions that must be satisfied for meaning to be found or to be adequately communicated can, of course, be specified. Traditional Indian (Vedāntic) thought properly recognizes at least four such conditions: (1) *ākāṃkṣā*, striving for completeness or absence of ambiguity—e.g., on hearing the sentence 'The daughter is here,' the hearer might very well want to know 'whose daughter?,' with the sentence being fully meaningful to him only upon his having that information; (2) *yogyatā* or compatibility between terms. In 'this idea weighs ten pounds' we have, in the absence of a code system, a series of words which fail to make sense because of the incompatibility of terms (or because of what we might now call "category-mistakes"); (3) *āsatti*, contiguity or proximity. For meaningful sentences to occur there must be a reasonable contiguity or proximity in space and time between the elements of the utterance; and (4) *tatparyya-jñāna*, or knowledge of what is intended so that the hearer is assured that the speaker means what his words mean as such. See *Vedāntaparibhāṣā*, chap. 4, trans. S. S. Suryanarayana Sastri (Adyar: Adyar Library, 1942), and D. M. Datta, *The Six Ways of Knowing* (Calcutta: University of Calcutta, 1960), pp. 308 ff.

Now, one could probably list many other conditions of this sort; but all of these conditions affect essentially our ability to determine the *degree* of meaning or clarity that is present in various utterances, and not with the recognition of intentionality itself. A warning might properly be recognized as a warning and in such a way as to enable one to act on it, and accordingly be meaningful, while at the same time it might be ambiguous in several minor respects. Because an utterance is meaningful once it is recognized for what it is in terms of its intentionality being exhibited does not, therefore, rule out the possibility of there being degrees of meaning or of clarity in various utterances. Two utterances can both be meaningful with one being more meaningful than the other.

18. Recognition of intentionality plays an equally important role in judgment. Suppose X presents Y with a complex mathematical proof and asks Y his opinion of it. It so happens that Y knows very little about mathematics; but he is something of an aesthete. He replies to X that he doesn't particularly like the spatial divisions between the lines and thinks the conclusion would be nicer if it were better centered on the page. X quite rightly rejects this judgment on the grounds that Y has missed the point of what a mathematical proof aims to do or be. Y is not responding to the symbols for what they are,

namely, a mathematical proof, but as they might for him constitute just a visual pattern or design.

19. This is not to suggest, however, that A-rules go to determine the meaning of utterances with equal intensity in all cases. Clearly they are of varying importance. Sometimes the contribution of A-rules to meaning can be so trivial as not to be noticed, as in many purely informational exchanges, like an announcer reading off the stock-market statistics of the day; at other times the contribution of A-rules may be crucial, as in many highly evocative utterances; e.g., when a poet recites his poem.

20. We have said that "a (rightly sensitive) respondent R *would* recognize I": we use the conditional form here in order to distinguish between X as potentially meaningful and X as actually meaningful; for it is certainly the case that we want to be able to talk about the meaning of utterances independently of their particular perlocutionary force in a given situation, while at the same time recognizing that "meaning" is a relational concept; that questions of meaning are questions only for consciousness. A rightly sensitive R is simply one who knows enough of the language of the utterance (whether it be a natural language, an abstract symbol-system, etc.) to recognize what the utterance is aiming to be, and is in a position to allow this knowledge to be brought into play, which means that he is able to attend to the utterance. A rightly sensitive R is precisely he who is able to actualize a potentially meaningful utterance in appropriate ways in appropriate situations.

21. John L. Austin, "Truth," *Proceedings of the Aristotelian Society,* Supplement, vol. 24 (1950). Reprinted in *Truth,* ed. George Pitcher (Englewood Cliffs, N.J.: Prentice-Hall, 1964), p. 175.

22. W. V. Quine, "Two Dogmas of Empiricism," *The Philosophical Review* 60 (1951), and in his *From a Logical Point of View* (Cambridge, Mass.: Harvard University Press, 1953), pp. 22–23.

Quine, of course, was set upon showing the complete inadequacy of the traditional empiricist distinction between synthetic and analytic statements. His arguments have been rather nicely met, though, by H. P. Grice and P. F. Strawson in their "In Defense of a Dogma," *The Philosophical Review* 65 (1956), and by other writers on analyticity such as Benson Mates, Jonathan Bennett, and R. M. Martin.

23. Alan R. White, *Truth* (Garden City, N.Y.: Doubleday & Co., 1970), p. 14.

24. Dorothy Walsh, "Literary and Linguistic Meaning,"*The British Journal of Aesthetics* 12 (1972): 325.

25. Cf. Moritz Schlick, "Facts and Propositions," *Analysis* 2 (1935).

26. White, *Truth,* p. 80.

27. David Mitchell, *An Introduction to Logic* (Garden City, N.Y.: Doubleday & Co., 1970), p. 129.

28. Aristotle, *Metaphysics* 1011.26.

29. Bertrand Russell, *The Problems of Philosophy* (New York: Oxford University Press, Galaxy Book, 1959), p. 127.

30. Ibid., p. 128.

31. Roderick Chisholm, *Theory of Knowledge* (Englewood Cliffs, N.J.: Prentice-Hall, 1966), p. 103.

32. The Liar paradox—that there is no way of getting at the truth of self-referring

statements such as ''What I am now saying is false,'' for if it were true then it would be false—still presents a problem for many logicians and epistemologists, with Chisholm being able to say that ''Any theory of truth should attempt to deal with the various versions of the ancient paradox called the 'Epimendes' or the Liar' '' (*Theory of Knowledge*, p. 107). Although Chisholm develops his view of truth with close reliance upon an Aristotelian correspondence conception, we would follow him in his method of dealing with the paradox, which is to argue that the paradox does not really express a proposition. Chisholm states that ''we may say of the beliefs and assertions giving rise to the paradox, that they are neither true nor false, for they are not beliefs or assertions with respect to any state of affairs, that that state of affairs exists'' (ibid., p. 109).

An ontological theory of truth likewise is not bothered by the Liar and similar paradoxes of the sort that inspired Tarski to develop the distinction between an object-language and a meta-language, for these paradoxes, we argue, are not propositions, the truth or falsity of which is at issue, precisely because they make no effort to present a fact: there is nothing in the paradox that can intelligibly report a state of affairs. In ''What I am now saying is false''—nothing, in *fact,* is being said.

33. Alfred Tarski, ''The Semantic Conception of Truth,'' *Philosophy and Phenomenological Research* 4 (1944). Reprinted in eds., H. Feigl and W. Sellars, *Readings in Philosophical Analysis* (New York: Appleton-Century-Crofts, 1949), p. 60.

34. Ibid., p. 54.

35. Ibid.

36. Rudolph Carnap gives this precise formulation of the semantic conception: ''The sentence S is true (in a given language L) if and only if there is a proposition, p, such that S designates p, and p.'' See his *Introduction to Semantics* (Cambridge, Mass.: Harvard University Press, 1942).

37. Tarski, ''The Semantic Conception,'' p. 57.

38. Ibid., p. 65.

39. See F. P. Ramsey, ''Facts and Propositions,'' *Proceedings of the Aristotelian Society,* Supplement, vol. 7 (1927).

40. White, *Truth,* p. 82. White, however, then presses his argument in the wrong direction when he attempts to refute the view ''that facts, like true statements, are linked only by logical relations, e.g. that facts imply each other.'' He says: ''On the contrary, facts, unlike true statements, have causal effects. It was the fact, not the true statement, that the train was diverted which made me late for my lecture'' (ibid., p. 83). But it is neither the fact nor the true statement that caused the lateness; it was the event or state of affairs itself.

41. P. F. Strawson, ''Truth,'' *Analysis* 9 (1949). Reprinted in *Truth,* ed. George Pitcher, p. 161.

42. Ibid., p. 165.

43. Austin, ''Truth,'' p. 169.

44. Ibid., p. 176.

45. Mitchell, *Introduction to Logic,* p. 118.

46. Paul Marhenke, ''Facts and Descriptive Reference,'' in *Studies in the Nature of Facts,* University of California Publications in Philosophy (Berkeley: University of California Press, 1932), 14:122.

47. Cf. Edward Erwin, *The Concept of Meaninglessness* (Baltimore and London: Johns Hopkins Press, 1970), pp. 88 ff.

48. George Lakoff, "Deep Language," Letter to Editor, *New York Review of Books*, 20, no. 1, p. 34.

49. This implies that the manner, style, expressive quality of an articulation is always relevant for determining meaning, even in those cases where a kind of dull clarity and precision is attained, as in weather reports; but it does not imply that expressive quality is always important for establishing truth in propositional language. The factuality of the proposition, as it were, is not controlled by the manner of its expression, although our ability to determine what that factuality is may very much be controlled by these qualitative factors.

50. Austin, "Truth," p. 174.

51. Brand Blanshard, *The Nature of Thought* (New York: Macmillan Co., 1940), 2:289.

52. Cf. H. Khatchadourian, *The Coherence Theory of Truth* (Beirut: 1961), pp. 13 ff.

53. Blanshard, *The Nature of Thought*, p. 291.

54. Ibid., p. 292.

55. A coherence theory of truth which is not dependent upon the metaphysics of idealism but which stresses logical entailment and consistency (without claiming an identity between thought and reality) has interestingly enough been developed in the modern positivist tradition. See Carl G. Hemple, "On the Logical Positivists' Theory of Truth," *Analysis* 2, no. 4 (1935).

56. See Norwood R. Hanson, "A Note on Statements of Fact," *Analysis* 13, no. 1 (1952), where he distinguishes "factual statements" or true propositions from "statements of fact" and argues that it is only the latter that is not capable of being false.

57. This view of what constitutes an adequate test for truth is similar in many ways (and yet is still different from) the view put forward in the classical Indian school of philosophy known as Advaita Vedānta. The advaitins argue that noncontradictoriness *(abādhitatva)* constitutes a sufficient ground for truth in judgments. Their notion, however, centers mainly on the possibility of something being replaced by something else because of a greater reality and value that something else may possess. It is thus what I have called a "subrating" process in which axiological considerations are closely interwoven with noetic concerns, and which is used primarily to establish different orders of being. (See my *Advaita Vedānta: A Philosophical Reconstruction* [Honolulu: The East-West Center, 1969], chap. 2.) *Abādhitatva* is not strictly a test for the truth of propositional language so much as it is part of a process which seeks to discriminate knowledge *(jñāna)* from both error *(mithyā-jñāna)* and ignorance *(avidyā; ajñāna)*.

Closely connected with this notion of noncontradictedness is the theory put forward in Advaita known as *svatahprāmānyavāda*, the theory of the intrinsic validity of knowledge. This theory argues explicitly for the self-evidential character of truth, stating as it does that any idea or proposition is taken by utterer and receiver to be valid until such time as it is shown to be false—to be contradicted. This means that the test for truth has indeed to do more with falsification than with verification. There is no way open to us, the advaitins argue, to get outside the process by which knowledge is acquired in order to verify any particular knowledge-claim. We can look only to the internal conditions for knowledge and truth and not to any external correspondence or utilitarian (or coherence) criterion. (See ibid., pp. 86 ff.)

CHAPTER IV

1. Nicholas Rescher, in his recent *The Coherence Theory of Truth* (Oxford: Clarendon Press, 1973), states, and presumably settles, the matter in his opening paragraph: "Philosophical theories in general deal exclusively with the truth of statements or propositions—or, derivatively, such complexes thereof as accounts, narrations, and stories. Other uses of 'true' in ordinary language . . . are beside the point of concern" (p. 1).

2. I understand the distinction between truth *as* being and the truth *of* being in these terms: by truth *as* being is meant truth as formally applying to reality, whatever in actuality reality might be; by the truth *of* being is meant precisely the way reality in fact is. To understand, explicate, relate the noetic character of truth *as* being is the task of epistemology, which asks what truth is; to discover the truth *of* being is the work of metaphysics (and any other substantive philosophic discipline, or science or art in their own ways), which asks what is the truth.

3. Scholastic philosophers also elaborated a twofold truth, but this was done in terms of marking off what was taken to be the appropriate domains of "faith" and "reason." Faith, a giving of assent to inevident truths, was for the supernatural, graceful content of revealed spirit; reason, the intellectual discovery of first principles and the demonstrating of truths that may follow from them, was for the world of our ordinary experience, and possibly for the "that," but not the "what," of the spiritual order. The two orders, when functioning properly, it was believed, never contradict one another. Any apparent contradiction, should it arise, would be attributed to the inadequacy of reason.

Now, this schema remains a dualism (however harmonious) between two kinds of truth. A level approach, on the other hand, would insist that no relation can be established between two incommensurable orders of truth. In fact, if the one were to exist positively as a content of consciousness, and not just formally as a concept, the other would cease to exist in the manner in which it was first taken to exist. If truth *as* being were fully realized as the truth *of* being, if, that is to say, consciousness were identical with reality, then individual beings in process—the domain of our ordinary experience—would no longer be as a content of consciousness and their truth at that time would be utterly irrelevant. This way of putting the nonrelation, as it were, between the two types of truth is similar in many ways to the manner in which in Indian thought, for both later Buddhist and Vedāntic traditions, a distinction is drawn between *paramārtha satya* and *samvṛti satya. Paramārtha satya* means the absolute truth of being which is void of distinction of any kind, and *samvṛti satya* means the relative or practical truths of our ordinary experience in the world. The former is, in actuality, the sole truth; when experienced it contradicts any other truth-claim by virtue of its overwhelming reality; from its standpoint, there are no other truths. In the Indian tradition, in short, it is because of the metaphysical nature of the truth of being—and not just the epistemological character of truth as being—that we have this twofold truth. I have suggested here, on the other hand, that a twofold truth can be acknowledged regardless of what reality in actuality is or is thought by us to be, simply because of the nature of the kind of truth that we do seek in our ordinary experience of individual beings.

4. Bertrand Russell, *The Problems of Philosophy* (New York: Oxford University Press, Galaxy Book, 1959), p. 119.

5. This does not mean that one must literally (either in actuality or in imagination) replace an inferior work by one that would be better for it—in which case only outstanding artists could contradict artworks—it means only that in falsification we recognize the need for the object as it is to be replaced by another within its own conditions and intentionality.

Bibliography

A rather complete bibliography on "truth" is available in Alan R. White's book *Truth* (Garden City, N.Y.: Doubleday & Co., 1970), pp. 130 ff. A select bibliography arranged by subheadings of the various main theories of truth is also available in George Pitcher, ed. *Truth* (Englewood Cliffs, N.J.: Prentice- Hall, 1964), pp. 113 ff. Following are some of the main sources referred to, directly or indirectly, in our text, many of which, due to our working with aesthetic and religious experience, as well as with propositional language, are not included in these bibliographies.

Acton H. B. "The Correspondence Theory of Truth." *Proceedings of the Aristotelian Society.* New series, 35 (1934–1935):177–194.

Austin, John. "Truth." *Proceedings of the Aristotelian Society.* Supplement, 24 (1950):111–128.

Ayer, A. J. "Truth." *Révue internationale de philosophie* 7, 25 (1953):183–200.

Black, Max. "The Semantic Definition of Truth." *Analysis* 8 (1948):49–63.

Blanshard, Brand. *The Nature of Thought.* 2 vols. New York: Macmillan Co., 1940. Chaps. 25–27.

Chisholm, Roderick. *Theory of Knowledge.* Englewood Cliffs, N.J.: Prentice-Hall, 1966. Chap. 7.

Dewey, John. "Propositions, Warranted Assertibility, and Truth." *Journal of Philosophy* 38 (1941).

Ducasse, C. J. *Truth, Knowledge and Causation.* London: Routledge & Kegan Paul, 1968.

Elliot, R. K. "Poetry and Truth." *Analysis* 27, 3 (January 1967).

Flew, Antony, and MacIntyre, Alasdair, eds. *New Essays in Philosophical Theology.* New York: Macmillan Co., and London: Student Christian Movement Press, 1955.

Heidegger, Martin. "On the Essence of Truth." Trans. R. F. C. Hull and Alan Crick. In Werner Brock, ed. *Existence and Being.* Chicago: Henry Regnery Co., 1949.

_____. *Platons Lehre von der Wahrheit. Mit einen Brief uber den "Humanismus."* Bern: A. Francke, 1947.

Hemple, Carl. "On the Logical Positivists' Theory of Truth." *Analysis* 2 (1935):49–59.

Hiriyanna, Mysore. "The Nyāya Conception of Truth and Error." *Indian Philosophical Studies,* I. Mysore: Kavyalaya Publishers, 1957.

Hofstadter, Albert. *Truth and Art.* New York: Columbia University Press, 1965.

Hook, Sidney, ed. *Religious Experience and Truth.* New York: New York University Press, 1961.

James, William. *Pragmatism.* New York: David McKay Co., 1907.

_____. *The Meaning of Truth.* New York: Longmans, Green and Co., 1909.

Jessup, Bertram E. "Truth as Material in Art." *The Journal of Aesthetics and Art Criticism* 4, 2 (Winter 1945):110–114.

Kneale, William. "Truths of Logic." *Proceedings of the Aristotelian Society.* New series, 46 (1945–1946):207–234.

Levi, Albert William. "Literary Truth." *The Journal of Aesthetics and Art Criticism* 24, 3 (Spring 1966):373–382.

Marhenke, P. "Belief and Facts." In *Studies in the Nature of Truth.* University of California Publications in Philosophy, no. 11. Berkeley: University of California Press, 1929. Pp. 119–148.

Mascall, Eric L. *Existence and Analogy.* London: Longmans, Green and Co., 1949.

Morgan, Douglas N. "Must Art Tell the Truth." *The Journal of Aesthetics and Art Criticism* 26, 1 (Fall 1967):17–27.

Pitcher, George, ed. *Truth.* Englewood Cliffs, N.J.: Prentice-Hall, 1964.

Price, Kingsley. "Is There Artistic Truth?" *The Journal of Philosophy* 46, 2 (May 1949):285–291.

Quine, W. V. *From a Logical Point of View.* Cambridge, Mass.: Harvard University Press, 1953. Chap. 1.

Ramsey, F. P. "Facts and Propositions." *Proceedings of the Aristotelian Society.* Supplement, 7 (1927):153–170.

Reid, Louis Arnaud. "Art, Truth and Reality." *The British Journal of Aesthetics* 4, 4 (October 1964):321–331.

Russell, Bertrand. *The Problems of Philosophy.* New York: Oxford University Press, 1959. [First published in 1912.] Chap. 12.

_____. *An Inquiry Into Meaning and Truth.* London: George Allen & Unwin, 1940.

Sartre, Jean-Paul. *Being and Nothingness.* Trans. Hazel Barnes. New York: The Philosophical Library, 1956.

Schlick, Moritz. "Facts and Propositions." *Analysis* 2 (1935):65–70.

Sesonske, Alexander. "Truth in Art." *The Journal of Philosophy* 53, 11 (May 1956):345–353.

Smith, Wilfred Cantwell. *A Human View of Truth.* In Studies in Religion/Sciences religieuses 1, 1 (1971).

Sparshott, F. E. "Truth in Fiction." *The Journal of Aesthetics and Art Criticism* 26, 1 (Fall 1967):3–7.

Strawson, P. F. "Truth." *Analysis* 9 (1949):83–97.

Tarski, Alfred. "The Semantic Conception of Truth." *Philosophy and Phenomenological Research* 4 (1944):341–375.

Tillich, Paul. *Dynamics of Faith.* New York: Harper & Row, 1958.

Walsh, Dorothy. "The Cognitive Content of Art." *The Philosophical Review* 52, 4 (September 1943):433–451.

White, Alan. *Truth.* New York: Doubleday & Co., 1970.

Zink, Sidney. "Poetry and Truth." *The Philosophical Review* 54, 2 (1945):132–154.

Index

✦ Production Notes

This book was designed by Roger J. Eggers and
typeset on the Unified Composing System by the
design and production staff of The University Press
of Hawaii.

The text and display typeface is Garamond No. 49.

Offset presswork and binding were done by Halliday
Lithograph. Text paper is Glatfelter P & S Offset,
basis 55.

Date Due